U.S. Fish & Wildlife Service

Statistical Guide to Data Analysis of Avian Monitoring Programs

Biological Technical Publication

BTP-R6001-1999

Nadav Nur
Point Reyes Bird Observatory, Stinson Beach, CA 94970

Stephanie L. Jones
U.S. Fish & Wildlife Service, Mountain-Prairie Region, Denver, CO 80225

Geoffrey R. Geupel
Point Reyes Bird Observatory, Stinson Beach, CA 94970

Authors
Nadav Nur
Point Reyes Bird Observatory
4990 Shoreline Hwy.
Stinson Beach, CA 94970-9701
415/868 1221
email: NadavNur@prbo.org

Stephanie L. Jones
Nongame Migratory Bird Coordinator
U.S. Fish & Wildlife Service, Mountain-Prairie Region
P.O. Box 25486 DFC
Denver, CO 80225
303/236 8145 ext. 608
email: Stephanie_Jones@fws.gov

Geoff Geupel
Point Reyes Bird Observatory
4990 Shoreline Hwy.
Stinson Beach, CA 94970-9701
415/868 1221
email: GGeupel@prbo.org

Suggested citation
Nur, N., S.L. Jones, and G.R. Geupel. 1999. A statistical
guide to data analysis of avian monitoring programs.
U.S. Department of the Interior, Fish and Wildlife
Service, BTP-R6001-1999, Washington, D.C.

Table of Contents

List of Tables and Figures

Tables

Figures

Preface

This Statistical Guide is intended to aid field biologists wishing to analyze data gathered in standardized monitoring programs for landbirds. It grew out of the needs expressed by the Western Working Group of *Partners in Flight*, and we thank the members of that group for providing the incentive to develop this document. It is not intended to replace good statistical texts, but to supplement them. We encourage readers, and especially users, of this Guide to forward their comments, corrections, and other advice to the senior author for incorporation into future versions of this Guide.

This work has been a contract between Point Reyes Bird Observatory and the U.S. Fish & Wildlife Service. This is PRBO Contribution 679.

References to commercial products does not imply endorsement.

Acknowledgments
We thank John R. Sauer, J. Scott Dieni, Ken Gerow, Daniel R. Petit, and Jon Bart for multiple reviews of earlier drafts; John Cornely, Barry Noon, Kathie Purcell, C.J. Ralph, Len Thomas, and Jerry Verner also provided helpful discussion and comments on an earlier draft of this document. The authors, not the above named reviewers, should be held responsible for any errors or outlandish opinions expressed here. We thank Jim Nichols for providing a helpful preprint. We thank the USFWS Nongame Coordinators: Tara Zimmerman, Bill Howe, Steve Lewis, Diane Pence, Richard Coon, Kent Wohl, together with Dan Petit and John Trapp, for support and encouragement. Special thanks to all the field biologists who took the time to assist us in doing this document and are out there doing the work, facing the challenges, and balancing the issues: Adrianna Araya, Grant Ballard, Sharon Browder, Mike Bryant, Claire Caldes, Lynn Clark, Paula Gouse, Ron Garcia, Todd Grant, Bill Haglan, Jeanne Hammond, Laura Hubers, Craig Hultberg, Beth Madden, Steve Martin, Bob Murphy, Lark Osborne, Fritz Prellwitz, Pam Rizor, Vickie Roy, Kelli Stone, Julian Wood, Kodiak and McDougall Jones and many more.

I. Introduction

This Guide is intended to provide guidance to field biologists wishing to analyze data collected on terrestrial bird populations, as part of an avian population monitoring program. A second objective is to provide information that will help biologists design such programs. The audience is similar to that for the *Handbook of Field Methods* (Ralph et al. 1993), the *Monitoring Bird Populations by Point Counts* (Ralph et al. 1995), and in many ways this *Statistical Guide to Data Analysis of Avian Monitoring Programs* can be a useful complement to the field methods handbook. At the same time, we feel this Statistical Guide can be of use to field biologists studying other organisms besides terrestrial birds. In our view, all field biologists will benefit from taking the equivalent of 2 or 3 semester courses in statistics and we assume that readers of this guide have completed at least this basic level in statistics.

This document is not intended to fill deficiencies in basic knowledge of statistics, nor is it a substitute for a good statistical text. Rather, this Guide is intended as a supplement to these texts. Our aim is to provide practical advice in the design and analysis of field ecological data and to provide timely information about current statistical computer programs. Two good statistical texts are provided by Neter et al. (1990) and Kleinbaum et al. (1988). Both of these texts are "intermediate" in level; that is, they assume the reader has had a basic, introductory course in statistics. Other texts by Snedecor & Cochran (1989), Sokal & Rohlf (1995) and Zar (1996) all provide a good, general statistical background. Intermediate level guides for practicing ecologists are provided by Crawley (1993), Bart and Notz (1996) and Bart et al. (1998). Noteworthy specialized statistical ecological texts include Ludwig & Reynolds (1988), Skalski & Robson (1992), and Draper & Smith (1981). The last two mentioned have many biological examples. Also see the informative review by Lancia et al. (1996).

Computer Programs
Computer programs for summarizing and analyzing data with general statistical packages are available, for many different levels, prices and target audiences. Ellison (1992) reviewed a number of general statistical packages, but that review is somewhat out of date. One versatile statistical and graphical package, available for DOS, Windows, and UNIX platforms, is Stata (StataCorp. 1999) (obtained from Stata Corporation, 702 University Drive East, College Station, TX 77840). Specialized computer software programs have been created to assist with analysis of capture/recapture data (used for analyses of survivorship, also population size); these are reviewed and summarized in this and additional specialized computer programs are mentioned in the respective sections of this Guide.

Recommended Monitoring Methods
A wide range of methods have been used to conduct avian monitoring, each tailored to meet a different set of objectives in the face of different constraints. This Guide does not address all methods that are available, especially those that are more widely used for research or inventory. Below is a short review of monitoring methods available, based on Butcher (1992) and Ralph et al. (1993). The reader is referred to these references (and others cited below) for additional information. Table 1 describes the variables measured and subjectively assesses the relative strengths and weaknesses of each method. "Strength" and "weakness" is assessed relative to the quality of the data gathered to meet the objective and we have not attempted to factor in cost per datum. Table 2 provides a list of monitoring objectives, monitoring methods and the typical time required by the various methods to achieve those objectives (from Geupel & Warkentin 1995). Descriptions of monitoring methods, their applications and comparisons, and their limitations can be found in Ralph and Scott (1981), Verner (1985), Butcher (1992), Ralph et al. (1993), Buckland et al. (1993) and Geupel & Warkentin (1995).

Methods
Area search—A method in which observers are allowed to roam for a fixed time in a specified area, usually 20 minutes per 3 hectare area (Loyn 1986, Slater 1994). This technique has a wide appeal to volunteers but standardization of data collection is difficult.

Table 1. Monitoring methods used in landbird population monitoring and their characteristics.
Methods are grouped under "survey" and "demographic." Positive or high level is denoted by "+", negative or low level denoted by "–" and partial level denoted by "+/–". Modified from Table 1 in Butcher (1992). "Color banding" is assumed to include nest-searching. "Rare" species refers to species that are locally (not just globally) rare.

Variables Measured	Survey				Demographic		
	Fixed distance	Spot map	Area Search	Variable distance	Mist net	Nest Search	Color banding
Index to abundance	+	+	+	+	+/–	+/–	+
Density	–	+	–	+	–	–	+
Survivorship (adult)	–	–	–	–	+	–	++
Productivity	–	–	–	–	+	+	+
Recruitment	–	–	–	–	+	–	+
Habitat Relations	+	+	+	+	+/–	+	+/–
Nest Site Characteristics	–	–	–	–	–	+	+
Predation/Parasitism	–	–	–	–	–	+	+
Individuals Identified	–	–	–	–	+	–	+
Breeding Status Known	–	+	–	–	+/–	+	+
General Characteristics							
Habitat specificity	+	+	+	+	+/–	+	+
Rare species measured	+	+/–	+	+/–	–	+/–	+/–
Canopy species measured	+	+	+	+	–	+/–	–
Area sampled known	+	+	+	+	+/–	+	+
Large area sampled	+	–	+	+	+/–	–	–
Use in non-breeding season	+	+/–	+	+	+	–	+

Table 2. Potential objectives of a monitoring program and typical number of years needed for a method to achieve results.
Actual number of years depends on study design and will vary depending on sample size (e.g., number of census stations, detection or capture rates, number of nests found). We assume that the priorities of the monitoring program reflect local or site-specific needs (adapted from Geupel & Warkentin 1995).

Objective	Method					
	Single Point Counts[a]	Repeat Pt. Counts[b]	Area Search[c]	Spot mapping	Mist netting[d]	Nest monitoring[d]
Inventory, species presence/absence	1	1	1	1	1	na
Inventory locally rare species	2-3	1-3	1-3	1-3	1-3	na
Determine species richness	2-3	1-3	1-3	1-3	na	na
Determine relative abundance	1-2	1-2	1-3	1-2	3-5	na
Determine species breeding status/seasonality	na	1-3	1-3	1-3	1-3	1-3
Determine population trend	6-10	5-9	10+	5-9	6-10	na
Determine productivity	na	na	na	na	1-3	1-2
Determine adult survivorship	na	na	na	3-5[e]	3-5	na
Determine life history traits	na	na	na	2-4	na	1-2
Habitat association or preference	1-2	1-2	1-2	1-3	na	1-2
Identify habitat features	4-6	3-5	3-5	2-4	na	1-2
Determine cause of pop. change	na	na	na	na	3+	3+

[a] Each point count censused one time in a season.

[b] Each point count censused 3 or more times in a season.

[c] Each plot censused 3 or more times in a season.

[d] Most authors/programs recommend this method in conjunction with population surveys.

[e] Possible if birds have been uniquely color-banded.

na Not applicable or not possible.

Methods for Assessing Abundance

Point counts—Fixed radius point counts are the basic method recommended for most monitoring studies, and are most widely used (Hutto et al. 1986, Ralph et al. 1993, Ralph et al. 1995). These can provide a cost-effective method of estimating the relative abundance of birds.

Line transects—Fixed-width transects can provide coverage of a greater area than point counts, but with fewer independent data points or replicates.

Variable distance methods—Estimating distance at which birds are detected can be incorporated into both point count and line transect surveys. Standardization of distance estimation may be difficult, as abilities to accurately estimate distances may vary greatly between observers.

Spot-mapping—Can provide good density information and information on many aspects of avian life history. It is expensive per data point and may be better applied to research projects or to high priority areas or species.

Demographic Methods

In general, demographic monitoring methods can be used to identify proximal causes of population declines and provide insight into causes of habitat associations. They can identify population problems prior to the detection of declines based on abundance surveys. Ultimately, these methods can be used to identify "source" or "sink" populations. However, these methods require much effort per station.

Constant effort mist-netting—Provides information on productivity and survivorship of populations, but is limited by area covered (which is generally unknown) and lack of habitat specificity. However, many species can be monitored at the same time, without expending extra effort.

Nest monitoring—Provides site-specific and habitat-specific information on productivity and reproductive status. Available personnel usually limit the number of plots that can be studied, and studying additional species normally requires increased effort.

Color-banding—When combined with nest monitoring, using unique color-band combinations to follow the fates of individuals will provide the most complete and unbiased measures of demographic parameters. However, it is the most intensive method of all. It is not a method recommended for general monitoring, but like spot-mapping, best suited for research projects or for high priority areas and species.

Statistical Terminology and Principles

The following is a selective review of some statistical terms relevant to a biologist conducting a monitoring study. Our intention here is to re-acquaint the reader with terms and principles that may have rested dormant for many years.

Accuracy—An estimator is accurate if it produces estimates that are, on average, close to the true value, i.e., without bias or with a minimum of bias. Accuracy is independent of precision (below). An estimate can be accurate but not precise, precise but not accurate, or both accurate and precise. The difficulty is that often the "true" value is unknown and therefore accuracy is difficult to judge, except for simulated data where an investigator knows the true values.

Bias—The difference between the average estimate (more precisely, the expected value of the estimate) and the true value. Bias is not the same as "error", rather it is one kind of error, systematic error. If an estimate is as likely to be an overestimate as it is to be an underestimate, the estimator in question is *unbiased*, even though there will always be error associated with an estimate. To minimize bias would, by definition, maximize accuracy.

Precision—Precision refers to the variability of the estimate: the smaller the variability (and thus the smaller the standard error) of the estimate, the greater the precision. As mentioned above, precision is independent of accuracy. An estimate can be very precise, but wildly inaccurate (i.e., strongly biased).

Type I and Type II errors—Rejecting the null hypothesis when it is correct is committing a Type I error. The probability of committing a Type I error is symbolized α [alpha] and is the significance level of a test of statistical inference. Accepting the null hypothesis when it is incorrect is committing a Type II error; the probability of making such an error is symbolized ß [beta].

Power—The probability of detecting a biological effect, if there is one. More precisely, power is the probability of rejecting the null hypothesis when the null hypothesis is incorrect. Normally, the null hypothesis is an hypothesis of no effect (i.e., no difference). Power is equal to 1–ß. Power cannot be calculated unless one specifies the alternative hypothesis: one must specify the magnitude of the effect or difference. A given test will have greater power the greater the magnitude of the effect, and conversely, the smaller the true difference between groups, the less the power to detect that difference for a given sample size. Power is discussed in greater depth in Chapter II of this Guide.

Poisson distribution—Among several discrete distributions (binomial, geometric, negative binomial), this distribution is one of the most likely to be encountered or utilized in ecological studies (Ludwig and Reynolds 1988). Many random processes, in which events occur independently of each other, in space or time, conform to a Poisson distribution. Suppose one set up a grid of 100 one-cm squares (10 cm × 10 cm). The number of rain drops falling per square in a short interval of time is likely to be Poisson-distributed. Suppose that in one minute, 100 rain drops fell on the 100 squares. If this process was indeed a Poisson process, then we would expect that in 1 minute, on average, 37 squares would receive 0 drops, 37 squares would receive 1 drop, 18 squares would receive 2 drops, and 8 squares would receive 3 or more drops. For a Poisson process, the mean of occurrences (per unit time or space, in the rain drop example = 1.0 drops per square per minute) will equal the variance of those occurrences. Thus, for a Poisson-distributed variable, only one parameter is specified.

Another useful distribution is the *binomial distribution*. If N independent trials were conducted and the probability of a "hit" (representing success, failure, death, etc.) on any one trial is p, then the number of hits in total is binomially distributed, with mean = Np, and Variance = $Np(1-p)$. As a result, variance is neither independent of the mean (as it is in the normal distribution) nor is it equal to the mean (as it is in the Poisson distribution); moreover, variance is maximized when $p = 1-p = 0.5$. As p approaches 0 or 1, the variance will shrink to zero. The binomial distribution is, for example, utilized in logistic regression (Chapter V). Note that the binomial distribution has two parameters, N and p. When the number of trials is large and the probability of a "hit", p, is low, then the binomial distribution can be approximated by the Poisson distribution.

Replicates—Replicates are independent repetitions or measurements within the experimental design. If repetitions are not independent then these "repeats" are sometimes referred to as pseudoreplicates (Hurlbert 1984, Bart et al. 1998). Suppose 100 point count stations in a given habitat type have been surveyed three separate times during the breeding season. The 300 data points obtained should not be treated as 300 replicates or samples, because bird data obtained on different days in the same season are not independent. Whether or not the 100 point count stations are independent or not is difficult to say *a priori*, but if spaced far enough apart (Ralph et al. 1995 recommend spacing of at least 250 m), so that the same individuals are not being counted at different stations, the 100 point count stations can be treated as independent. Assuming independence

among adjacent point count stations, and if the 100 point count stations were divided evenly among 4 habitats, then there would be 25 replicates.

As far as the three repeats per point count station are concerned, one can average the data, select the repeat with the highest score for each individual species, or sum the data from each of the three visits. If one wished to compare results among the three visits (e.g., asking whether there was a seasonal, within-year trend), one can analyze the 300 observations, using "point count station" as a categorical variable to be controlled for; this is an example of a repeated-measures design, in which "point count station" is a blocking variable.

Independence of observations—This is an important issue in statistical analysis, and is often misunderstood. To start, what is required are that outcomes be independent from one observation to another, after controlling for factors or variables that might be influencing the outcome. Suppose the point count stations have been spaced 100 m apart on transects of 1 km length. An investigator might not feel comfortable in treating observations from different stations on the same transect as being independent of each other. One solution would be to classify the transect as the unit of observation, i.e., pooling data from all point count stations on the same transect, and analyze data accordingly. Another solution would be to include in the analysis a "transect effect." This would control for the fact that stations on the same transect are more likely to be similar in outcome than are stations on different transects. In this way one can investigate differences among and within transects.

A second point is that the independence refers to the outcome, not the independent variables or factors. Suppose one related bird species richness to vegetation. As long as bird species richness varies independently from station to station (after controlling for various factors), it would not matter that all stations on a transect shared some of the same vegetation characteristics. In other words, there is no requirement that vegetation characteristics be independent from one observation unit to another.

General Considerations of Study Design

General study design considerations will apply to most monitoring techniques and studies. Neter et al. (1990) provides a good discussion of experimental design, also see Skalski & Robson (1992) and Crawley (1993); those wishing more detail can consult specialized texts such as Hicks (1982). A helpful and interesting discussion of the issues and the process for designing an avian monitoring study on one site such as a National Wildlife Refuge is given in Johnson (In Press). In this section, we discuss some general points concerning design of a study. Later when discussing each methodology in turn (point counts, mist-netting and nest-monitoring), we return to questions of design. Throughout this Guide, the use of "station" refers to one independent monitoring site, e.g., one point count station (if observations are deemed independent of other stations), one line transect, one mist-netting array, one nest-monitoring plot, etc. It is important to correctly determine the unit of analysis early in the study design.

Design—The first and most important consideration in designing a study is its objectives. Statistical inference (in particular, tests of statistical significance) may be of little interest, in which case statistical power need not be considered in determining the sample size needed. A biologist may instead wish to monitor a particular area mainly as a descriptive tool. If data are gathered in a standardized fashion (Ralph et al. 1993), the data from one area can contribute to regional or national monitoring programs, which likely have statistical inference as an objective. In many cases the number of stations will be limited by available resources or by the physical areas of interest. Some field biologists will be able to establish one, or at most, a couple of demographic monitoring stations (e.g., one mist-net array or one nest-monitoring plot). In those cases placement of the station will usually be constrained by the location and size of the habitat of interest, by the density of the species of special concern, or be centered on the location of the habitat or species of interest.

Data from just a single demographic monitoring station may be valuable for several reasons: 1. the data provide a description of temporal patterns, which data can be combined with other sources of data, 2. the data can allow statistical tests of trends over time, given sufficient number of years of data collection (possibly 10 years or more for a single station), and 3. the data can be combined with data from other monitoring stations.

Not every monitoring program needs to have hypothesis testing as its goal from the outset. A monitoring program may be able to collect valuable data that can later be analyzed (by itself or as part of a larger study), and that analysis would surely include hypothesis testing and tests of statistical significance. But it is pointless to erect contrived hypotheses before data collection has begun, simply in order to justify the establishment of a monitoring program. After data have been collected, the investigator will have a much better idea of how to formulate meaningful hypotheses. This point does not apply to experimental studies, where explicit hypothesis formulation is an essential ingredient to a successful study.

Assuming statistical inference is an important consideration, one needs to determine whether the objective is to determine trends through time, establish bird-habitat relationships, compare effects of different treatments, or other possible objective. Choice of objective will influence questions of sample size and allocation of stations (see Randomization below).

Assuming that statistical inference is a goal, the question of necessary sample size needs to be related to *statistical power*, i.e., the ability to detect an effect if there is one. Statistical power is an elusive concept in part because it is arbitrary. Calculations of sample size in the past have used power values ranging from 50% to 95%. Clearly, the greater the desired power, the greater the sample size necessary to achieve that power. Generally, this Guide uses values of 50% and 80%. In designing a study one would not ordinarily consider 50% power to be adequate and we do not recommend a study be designed to achieve 50% power. Nevertheless 50% power presents a useful level for *a posteriori* investigations, where someone has already collected these data and the biologist wishes to consider the statistical power of the data to detect effects of interest. Conversely, in designing a study, 80% power is a commonly used and often-recommended benchmark, but it is nothing more than a benchmark.

Power calculations and sample size calculations both rely on the presumed magnitude of the effect in question. Clearly, the greater the presumed effect (e.g., the greater the difference between the two groups), the greater the power will be to detect that effect, and, conversely, the smaller the necessary sample size to detect an effect at a specified power. The difficulty here is that the true difference between groups is unknown, and furthermore one cannot necessarily use the observed magnitude of an effect (e.g., observed difference between two groups) as the criterion for judging power.

It is easy to fall into the trap of estimating power, retrospectively, using the observed magnitude of an effect, and several general statistical packages appear to encourage users to do so, without appropriate warnings (discussed in Thomas and Krebs 1997). The problem is that if a statistically significant effect is found, one would not normally calculate power retrospectively. If the investigator looks for an effect and finds there is one, then there is little need to determine the probability of having found that effect. Therefore, retrospective power calculations are usually pursued only when no significant effect is detected. But given that no effect was detected (statistically), it could be because the observed magnitude of an effect was substantial, but power was weak, or because the observed magnitude of an effect was small, even negligible. However, power will always be low to detect a negligible effect. It is not very informative to calculate that, given the negligible effect observed, yes, one's power to detect a negligible effect is negligible. Thus, to be useful, retrospective power analysis requires that only effects of *a priori* interest be examined. In other words, in conducting power analysis, *the magnitude of the effect of interest needs to be fixed independently of the data at hand*. The biologist must decide what is the magnitude of an effect worth considering; this is a biological, not a statistical, issue that is sometimes difficult to settle.

Randomization—Randomization is an important part of experimental design, owing to the work of Sir Ronald Fisher in the early 20th century. Randomization is used to combat biases that can undermine survey and experimental studies. The most important bias concerns assignment to treatments. By randomizing assignment to treatment (e.g., grazed vs. ungrazed), extraneous differences among experimental units can be minimized. Even here one would likely use randomization subject to constraint. Suppose one had five land units, each one that can be divided into four plots. Randomly choosing treatment for the 20 plots could result in an unbalanced design. Instead, one can randomly choose treatment, subject to the constraint of 10 plots for each treatment. An even better design would use land unit as a blocking variable. Within each block (here, land unit), one randomly assigns treatment to plots, with the constraint that there must be two plots for each treatment. Of course, in many studies assignment to treatment is not always under the investigator's control.

Randomization should also be applied to minimize other types of bias, if feasible. If two treatments are being compared using point counts, using two observers, one should not assign one observer to conduct point counts in treatment A and the other observer to conduct point counts in treatment B. In this case, observer identity and the effect of the treatment would be confounded. Instead, the two treatments should be divided between the two observers, as randomly or equitably as possible. Another bias concerns order of observation. If several plots are to be visited each day, one should not visit the plots in the same order each time, but should vary the order. It is not usually feasible to

visit point count stations in a random order, but one can usually randomize the starting point on each visit.

The final source of bias concerns inclusion in a study. The sample to be studied will likely be the most representative of the population in question if it is randomly selected; however, this is often not feasible. Nevertheless, we recommend incorporating some randomness into every study. For example, one could lay out a grid of point count stations, centered on a randomly selected starting point as suggested by Sauer (1998). This approach can be adapted for those setting up transects of point count stations: the starting point for a transect can be randomly selected among a subset of possible points. Another approach is to set up a grid of possible stations and then randomly determine whether or not to include individual stations in the study. Hutto et al. (1996) and Hutto and Paige (1995) provide other suggestions for randomizing point count stations across broad areas.

Analysis of Vegetation and Habitat Characteristics

Data on vegetation and habitat features can play an important role in avian monitoring studies. These data can be gathered at different scales and in many different ways. Methods of vegetation data collection are described in many publications, including Ralph et al. (1993), the BBIRD program protocol (Martin et al. 1997), and Hays et al. (1981). One of the most influential vegetation assessment protocols developed for use with bird studies is by James and Shugart (1970), with modifications by Noon (1981). The analyses of vegetation data collected in conjunction with point counts and nest-monitoring are discussed in the appropriate sections.

Vegetation data can be collected and analyzed at several different scales. The broadest is habitat classification and is qualitative (categorical) rather than quantitative. This level includes most vegetation maps and can be used to select the vegetation types for study. The next broadest scale is the "stand" level. This scale is commonly used to ground-proof aerial photographs and, depending on methods, to construct bird-habitat (or bird-vegetation) correlations, making use of point count and line transect data. The third scale involves vegetation used to characterize the study area at a smaller scale than the first methods, often within a radius of 11.28 m following James and Shugart (1970). In some studies, plots are centered on nests or other sites of bird use ("use sites"), while others ("non-use sites") are randomly placed for comparison within the study area. This scale allows data that are more quantitative in nature to be collected, compared to other scales. Examples of studies using this scale are Knopf et al. (1988) and Larson & Bock (1986). This scale provides a good means to establish bird-habitat relationships; such data can be gathered quickly, accurately and efficiently. The finest scale of vegetation measurement is around the nest, nest plant or other micro-habitat features (Martin & Roper 1988; Martin et al. 1997).

Currently there is little agreement among biologists on the methods, and even the scale, of vegetation data collection needed to correlate with bird abundance, habitat needs, distribution and behavior. Therefore, it is not possible at this time to recommend a single approach for analysis of vegetation data since the data analytic approach will depend on how the data were collected.

II. Assessment of Abundance and Species Composition Using Point Counts

Several techniques have been used for estimating abundance of birds (Verner 1985, Bibby et al. 1992, Butcher 1992, Skalski & Robson 1992, Buckland et al. 1993, Greenwood 1996, Lancia et al. 1996). In the past, two widely used and promoted methods have been point counts and line-transects (Ralph & Scott 1981, Buckland et al. 1993). Capture/recapture data is a third method used to estimate populations (Greenwood 1996, Lancia et al. 1996). Following the recommendations of the National Monitoring Working Group of *Partners in Flight* (Butcher 1992) and Ralph et al. (1993) and Ralph et al. (1995), we restrict our attention to point counts. Line-transects can also yield valuable data regarding population abundance and species composition; however, the design and analysis of transect data is beyond the scope of this Guide (Ralph & Scott 1981, Buckland et al. 1993). We assume that data will be collected using fixed radius point counts, as described in Ralph et al. (1993), rather than unlimited distance point counts or variable distance point counts (Ralph & Scott 1981).

Throughout this Guide we discuss how to analyze data gathered in a typical monitoring program and then discuss design of monitoring programs, especially sample size. Ideally, one should first put careful thought into designing a monitoring program before data collection and analysis. However, here we discuss data analysis first in order to give the reader a better idea of what sorts of data can be gathered and what are some inferences that can be drawn from data collected in a monitoring program.

Analysis

Point count data have commonly been analyzed with respect to 1. relative abundance, 2. species richness, 3. species diversity and 4. community similarity. An alternative to the analysis of relative abundance, has been 5. the analysis of species presence/absence (i.e., a species is scored as 1 if one or more individuals are detected, and 0 if otherwise). (We recommend not using the term "frequency of occurrence" to characterize such analyses, because of ambiguity of this terminology.) However, from the point of maximizing statistical power, the analysis of relative abundance (i.e., number of individuals detected per station) is to be

preferred to an analysis of presence/absence. The latter discards information, leading to a loss of statistical power. On this point we are in agreement with Dawson (1981),

> "[E]ither frequency of occurrence or average number [per station] is adequate measure for species which occur usually as one or none in each counting unit. On the other hand, frequency becomes an increasingly insensitive measure for species found in larger numbers."

Presence/absence may be very helpful as a descriptive tool. That is, it may be informative to state that a species was present at 40% of stations in habitat x and 60% of stations in habitat y. Another advantage of presence/absence data is that some analytic methods can be used for such data but not for total detections. For example, logistic regression can be used with presence/absence, but not with total detections. Logistic regression is discussed in more detail in Chapter V and an example is provided below of the analysis of presence/absence data. Nevertheless, more sophisticated variants on logistic regression can use total detections (e.g, "ordered logistic regression", StataCorp. 1999). Also, Poisson regression, an analytic method that has much in common with logistic regression, can analyze total detections (Kleinbaum et al. 1988). As its name implies, Poisson regression assumes that the number of detections per station is Poisson-distributed, but some software (e.g., EGRET) includes the capability of testing this assumption (and modifying the analysis if data do not conform to this assumption).

Relative abundance is analyzed as number of detections per unit area. The number of individuals are determined at each point count station and this datum can be entered into regression analyses or analysis of variance (ANOVA). Results from several point count stations can be averaged to produce a summary statistic (Example 1). If a point count station is surveyed more than once per season, one can either sum the number of detections over all point count surveys or calculate an average number per point-count survey. As long as each station is surveyed the same number of times (e.g., three times), the two measures (average vs. sum) will differ only by a constant, in this case, three. A third commonly used method is to use the maximum number of detections over the course of the three surveys. In analyzing relative abundance these three methods can be expected to yield similar patterns.

The number of individuals detected at a point count station is a function of the absolute abundance and the probability of detecting an individual (given that it is present). Analyses of relative abundance assume that differences in detectability can be ignored, for the purposes of the study. In contrast, variable distance methods (often referred to as distance sampling; Buckland et al. 1993) attempt to estimate detectability. The assumption that differences in detectability are unimportant should be kept firmly in mind when considering surveys of relative abundance. Recent studies confirm that detectability is influenced by a number of different factors (Buckland et al. 1993, McShea & Rappole 1997, Gutzwiller & Marcum 1997).

Absolute abundance. Point count data are often used to determine relative abundance; however, absolute abundance may be estimated using variable distance methods (Buckland et al. 1993, Ramsey & Scott, 1981). An important assumption of variable distance methods is that at the center point of the observation, all individuals are detected (i.e., detectability = 100%). It is possible to relax this assumption if, instead, the true absolute density can be *independently* determined at the center point, but this is often not feasible. A second important assumption is that individuals do not move towards or away from the observer *before being detected*. Buckland et al. (1993) provide extensive discussion of these and other assumptions. The same authors have developed a program DISTANCE that carries out such analyses (Laake et al. 1993, Web site: <http://www.ruwpa.st-and.ac.uk/distance/>).

Species richness is analyzed as total number of species detected. A total can be calculated for each point count station, or for each group of point count stations (Example 1).

There are a plethora of indices for *species diversity* (Magurran 1988, Ludwig & Reynolds 1988). The utility of diversity indices has been strongly questioned by some (Verner & Larson 1989), and their use has limitations. It has been argued that species richness, a component of species diversity, is more easily and more accurately measured. Species richness is highly correlated with species diversity and can be interpreted more clearly (Verner & Larson 1989). An example of the value of a diversity index (but one that is admittedly extreme) is a comparison of two communities, each containing five species and each with a total of 100 individuals.

Community A contains 96 individuals of species 1 and 1 individual of each of the other 4 species; community B contains 20 individuals of each of five species. Which community is more diverse? If one feels that both are equally diverse, then species richness is all one needs to take into account. However, if one's view is that community B is more diverse, because its bird community is more heterogeneous, then one is justified in using a diversity index. However, keep in mind that more assumptions are required to estimate diversity than species richness. In particular, calculations of species diversity assume that relative abundance is accurately estimated and ignores the differences in detectability among species that can skew estimates of relative abundance.

The most widely used diversity index is referred to as Shannon's index, or as the Shannon-Wiener index or the Shannon-Weaver index (Krebs 1989). Shannon's index, which is derived from information theory, reflects both species richness and evenness of distribution among species present. An equation for the Shannon index, using natural logarithms (ln) is:

$$H' = \sum_{i=1}^{i=S} (p_i)(\ln p), \ \ i = 1, 2, \ldots S$$

where S = number of species in the sample, and p_i is the proportion of all individuals belonging to the *i*th species. The original Shannon index was calculated in terms of logarithm base 2, and thus H' was expressed in terms of bits; however, it is more common and more convenient to use natural logarithms, as we have done above. A useful transformation of H' is given by $e^{H'}$, which has been labeled N_1 (MacArthur 1965).

N_1 expresses diversity in terms of species instead of bits and thus is easier to interpret. N_1 provides the number of species that would, if each were equally common, yield the same H' value as the actual sample. For example, suppose there are 3 species, 20 of species A, 20 of species B and 10 of species C. Using the above equation, H' = 1.055 and N_1 = 2.87. These three species, in their uneven distribution, yield the same diversity value as would 2.87 species of equal abundance. A comparison of species richness (= S = 3) with N_1 (= 2.87) gives us a measure of evenness of species distribution. That is the species distribution is maximally even when S = N_1.

For a fixed S, the maximum diversity (H_{max}) is equal to $-\ln(1/S) = \ln(S)$ and therefore the ratio of observed diversity to maximum diversity is a measure of evenness (E): $E = H'/H_{max} = H'/\ln S$

Table 3. Example of data from point count observations conducted at three point count stations, three times during the breeding season.

A. Results by species. "A, A" indicates two individuals of species A were seen, "A, A, A" indicates three individuals, "A, B, C" indicates one individual of three species, etc.

Point Count Station	Survey Number	Species Observed	Number of Individuals	Species Richness
1	1	A, A, B, C	4	3
1	2	B, B, C, D	4	3
1	3	A, C, D, E	4	4
2	1	B, B, B, C	4	2
2	2	B, B, D	3	2
2	3	B, B, F	3	2
3	1	B, C, C, D	5	3
3	2	B, C, E, F, F	5	4
3	3	B, C, E, F, F, G	6	5

B. Summarization of data from Table 4A.

Point Count Station	Average Number Individuals	Cumulative Species Richness	Ecological Species Diversity[1]	Eveness = E
1	4.0	5	4.69	0.960
2	3.33	4	2.56	0.678
3	5.0	6	5.24	0.924
Average	4.11	5.0	3.86	0.839
Cumulative	12.33	7	5.55	0.881

[1] Shannon's index expressed as N_1

(Examples 1 and 2). If some species are more detectable than others this will bias one's measure of diversity, either upwards or downwards. If the Shannon index is calculated for a number of samples, the indices themselves will be normally distributed, making it possible to use parametric statistics to compare sets of samples using diversity indices (Magurran 1988). Further techniques for the analysis of diversity patterns are described in Magurran (1988) and Pielou (1975).

Example 1:
Calculation of Summary Statistics
The following is a simple and hypothetical example of data collected using point counts (Table 3). Observations were made at 3 point count stations at 3 different times during the breeding season. Species are uniquely identified by a single letter (A, B, C, etc.).

From these data, summary statistics can be calculated, first of all summing (or averaging) across the three survey periods, and then summing (or averaging) across the three point count stations whose data have already been summed over the 3 survey periods. Such a summarization is shown in Table 3B.

The results shown in Table 3A for each point count station can be used in a statistical analysis (e.g., regression or ANOVA) (Example 3). The biologist may also summarize results for a group of point count stations characterized by an important similarity, e.g., all stations at a specific site, or all stations in a specific habitat on a refuge, or other unit of interest.

The row titled "*Average*" in Table 3B (second from the bottom), simply averages the results from point count stations 1-3. The row titled "*Cumulative*" (bottom) shows the total number of individuals seen at the 3 point count stations (a measure of abundance), the total species richness for the 3 stations, and the species diversity as measured for all 3 stations taken together. Thus, the average station had 5 species, but the three stations together had 7 different species. For average number of individuals seen per point count survey, the "Cumulative" value is simply three times that of the "Average" value (i.e., $12.33 = 4.11 \times 3$). Thus the only difference between these two measures is that in one case one sums the number of individuals and divides by the number of point count stations and in the other case one sums and does not divide. Any statistical results will be identical whichever measure of individuals detected is used, except for a constant (in this case, 3, the number of point count stations).

In contrast to measures of abundance, *Average species richness* and *Cumulative species richness*, will generally not be so simply related to each other. At one extreme average species richness will equal cumulative species richness where there is complete overlap of species at each point count station. At the other extreme, cumulative species richness will be three times that of average species richness (assuming one is summarizing data from three point count stations) provided there is no species overlap at any point count station. Reality will usually fall somewhere in between. Either way of summarizing species richness can be justified. The same holds for species diversity; the average diversity (per point count station) and the diversity of the group of point count stations are both legitimate ways to characterize diversity.

_____

Community Similarity Indexes

Another method of comparing communities is to measure the degree of association or similarity in community composition between sites or samples. For example, two sites may be identical in species richness, but both have completely different species. For this purpose, a wide range of similarity indices have been developed (Magurran 1988). Two such indices that are widely used and that rely only on presence/absence data are the Jaccard index and Sorensen index (Krebs 1989):

Jaccard $\qquad C_j = \dfrac{j}{a+b-j}$

Sorenson $\qquad C_s = \dfrac{2j}{a+b}$

where j = the number of species found at both site A and B, a = the number of species in site A and b = the number of species found in site B. These indices are designed to equal 1 where the species from the two sites are the same and 0 if the sites have no species in common. Example 2 and Table 4 provide an example of a calculation of Jacard and Sorenson similarity coefficients.

One of the advantages to these indices is their simplicity, but the indices do not account for differences in the abundance of species. All species count equally in the equation whether they are abundant or rare. For this reason, *quantitative* indices of similarity have much appeal as an alternative. Again, many such indices have been developed (Magurran 1988, Krebs 1989). Here we just mention one of the simplest, the Renkonen

index, also called the Percentage Similarity index. The formula for the Renkonen index (P) is:

$$P = \sum_{i=1}^{i=S} \text{minimum} \, (p^A_i, p^B_i)$$

where p^A_i is the percentage of species i in sample A and p^B_i is the percentage of species i in sample B and S is the number of species found in either sample. With no overlap between samples the index equals 0, with complete similarity the Renkonen index equals 100%. Table 4 provides an example of the Renkonen index.

_____

Example 2:
Calculation of Community Similarity Indices

The following is an simplified example of data collected using point counts (Table 4). Observations were pooled using the highest number counted during 3 different surveys in the breeding season, and pooled across 5 paired treatment-control plots (modified from Dieni 1996). Community similarity and diversity indices can be calculated and comparisons made using these data.

The row titled "number of individuals" in Table 4 is the sum of the total number of individuals counted in each site. The columns titled "p^a" and "p^b" are the proportion of each species in the total; i.e., the number of individuals divided by the total number of individuals for that site. The calculation of Jaccard's index is the number of species in common (j) to both sites divided by the difference between the sum of the number of species in each site minus the number in common. Sorenson's index is 2 times j divided by the summation of the number of species in both sites.

Other indices may also be informative including the Renkonen index which is calculated by taking the summation of the minimum of either p^a or p^b. Other examples of the calculations of indices that may be useful are shown in Table 4.

_____

Linear Regression

To introduce linear regression, and provide a simple example of trend analysis we consider the following.

_____

Example 3:
An Example of Simple Regression

Black-headed Grosbeaks (*Pheucticus melanocephalus*) have been surveyed at the Palomarin station of Point Reyes National Seashore during the breeding season for many years. Here we present data from 1980-1992 (13 years) and wish to

Table 4. Calculation of diversity, similarity and evenness indices using total bird detections across sites in burned and unburned aspen (*Populus tremuloides*) stands in Wyoming (modified from Dieni 1996).

Species	Number of Individuals		Statistical Transformations				
	Burned	Control	Minimum p^a or p^b	p^a	$p^a \ln p^a$	p^b	$p^b \ln p^b$
Red-tailed Hawk	2	0	0.000	0.004	−0.021	0.000	0.000
American Kestrel	1	0	0.000	0.002	−0.012	0.000	0.000
Northern Flicker	36	20	0.036	0.068	−0.182	0.036	−0.119
Western Wood-Pewee	21	39	0.040	0.040	−0.128	0.070	−0.186
Dusky Flycatcher	13	9	0.016	0.024	−0.091	0.016	−0.066
Tree Swallow	47	29	0.052	0.089	−0.215	0.052	−0.153
Clark's Nutcracker	3	0	0.000	0.006	−0.029	0.000	0.000
Black-capped Chickadee	13	18	0.024	0.024	−0.091	0.032	−0.110
White-breasted Nuthatch	0	3	0.000	0.000	0.000	0.005	−0.028
Red-breasted Nuthatch	1	6	0.002	0.002	−0.012	0.011	−0.049
House Wren	127	142	0.239	0.239	−0.342	0.254	−0.348
Hermit Thrush	0	1	0.000	0.000	0.000	0.002	−0.011
American Robin	38	47	0.072	0.072	−0.189	0.084	−0.208
Warbling Vireo	163	199	0.307	0.307	−0.363	0.355	−0.368
Orange-crowned Warbler	14	40	0.026	0.026	−0.096	0.071	−0.189
Brewer's Blackbird	3	0	0.000	0.006	−0.029	0.000	0.000
Western Tanager	2	2	0.004	0.004	−0.021	0.004	−0.020
Pine Siskin	33	3	0.005	0.062	−0.173	0.005	−0.028
American Goldfinch	1	0	0.000	0.002	−0.012	0.000	0.000
Cassin's Finch	13	2	0.004	0.024	−0.091	0.004	−0.020
Number of individuals	531	560					
Number of species	18	15					
Number of species in common (j)	13						
Summations			0.827	1.0	−2.095	1.0	−1.903
Jaccard (C_j)		0.650					
Sorenson qualitative (C_s)		0.788					
Renkonen index (P)			0.827				
Shannon diversity (H)						2.095	1.903
Shannon evenness (E)						0.725	0.703
Shannon maximum value (H_{max})						2.890	2.708

determine if there has been a trend for numbers to increase or decrease during this period.

Keep in mind four key assumptions of linear regression analysis:

1. Normality of residuals

2. Homoscedasticity; that is, there are no systematic differences in variance of residuals

3. Independence of the outcome variable (i.e., independence of residuals), and

4. That we are interested in testing the hypothesis (H_A) that there is some sort of linear relationship between dependent and independent variable. In this case, the hypothesis is that bird abundance is decreasing or increasing with time, in a linear fashion.

Note that assumptions 1-3 refer to residuals, i.e., the difference between the observed value of the dependent (i.e., outcome) variable and the predicted value from a regression model, we have to fit a regression model before we can evaluate the residuals. Figure 1 shows observed data and fitted regression lines for this example, for log-transformed data (Figure 1A), and for untransformed data (Figure 1B). The log transformation is commonly used in analyses of linear models (e.g., regression and ANOVA; additional examples below). There are two reasons for using a logarithmic transformation:

Figure 1A. Trend, log-linear, P=0.001
Black-headed Grosbeak, Palomarin 1980-1992

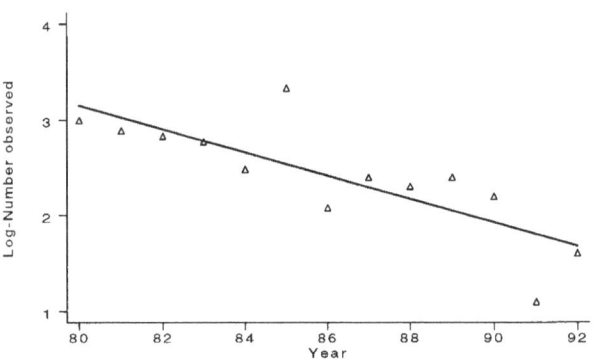

Figure 1B. Trend, linear—no transformation, P=0.004
Black-headed Grosbeak, Palomarin 1980-1992

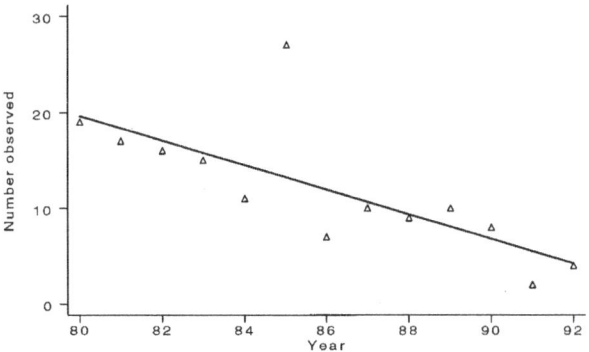

Figure 1. A. Linear trend in log(number Black-headed Grosbeaks observed) in relation to year (1980 to 1992), (statistical analysis in Table 5A). Triangles indicate log(number observed) in each year; solid line indicates best-fitting trend using linear regression analysis. The trend depicted is a log-linear trend. B. As in A. but numbers observed are untransformed. Statistical analysis in Table 5B; trend depicted is a linear trend. Note that trend line fits observations better for log-transformed data (Figure 1A) than for untransformed data (Figure 1B); e.g., with a higher R^2 0.637 vs. 0.545.

1. Linear models assume additivity, but the relationship between the dependent variable and an independent variable may be multiplicative, i.e., with an increase of each unit in x, y increases by a constant proportion. Exponential growth or decline of a population is a good example of a multiplicative model. In this case, we may wish to fit a model in which Black-headed Grosbeak numbers increase or decrease by $d\%$ per year; our objective is to estimate the value d, and test whether it is significantly different from zero.

By taking logarithms, one can convert a multiplicative relationship,

$$y = ab^x,$$

into an additive relationship,

$$\log(y) = \log(a) + (\log(b))(x).$$

What was once a multiplicative relationship can be rewritten in an additive form,

$$y' = a' + b'x.$$

2. The logarithmic transformation can often normalize residuals (as shown below), thus conforming to an important assumption of regression analysis, as well as of ANOVA, ANCOVA, and similar analysis.

A regression analysis on the log-transformed data is appropriate, but before doing so, we present typical output from STATA (Table 5) from a regression analysis with annotated comments (numbers below correspond to numbers on the output). Table 5A shows analysis of log-transformed data; Table 5B shows analysis of untransformed data.

1. Sums of Squares ("SS" in Table 5), degrees of freedom ("df"), and Mean Squares ("MS") are provided for the model being examined. This output is usually of greater interest in ANOVA than in regression analyses. Sums of squares are included in R^2 and R^2a (#3, below). "Model" refers to independent variables (in this case, only one) and does not include the "constant" term.

2. The F statistic ("F") for the entire model (excluding the constant) is shown, and the P-value associated with that statistic ("Prob >F"). The degrees of freedom of the numerator (the first term within the parentheses) equals the number of parameters in the model, excluding the constant. If a model includes linear trends for two independent variables, the numerator df is equal to 2. If the model, instead, includes quadratic and linear terms for a single independent variable then the numerator df is also equal to 2. If the model includes linear trends for two independent variables and their interaction, then the numerator df is equal to 3, and so on.

The overall P-value, while of some interest, should be of less concern than P-values for individual terms. A model which contains one very significant independent variable and one insignificant independent variable can generate a highly significant overall P-value, though such a model

Table 5A. Linear regression analysis of number of Black-headed Grosbeaks, breeding season, log-transformed (=ltotbrs) vs. year.

Source	① SS	df	MS			
Model	2.71854704	1	2.71854704	Number of obs	=	13
Residual	1.54865857	11	.140787142	② F (1, 11)	=	19.31
				Prob > F	=	0.0011
Total	4.26720561	12	.355600468	③ Rsquare	=	0.6371
				Adj Rsquare	=	0.6041
				④ Root MSE	=	.37522

ltotbrs	Coef.	Std. Err.	t	P>|t|	⑤ [95% Conf. Interval]	
year	.1222173	.0278129	4.394	0.001	.183433	.0610016
_cons	245.1384	55.23646	4.438	0.001	123.5637	366.713

Table 5B. Linear regression analysis of number of Black-headed Grosbeaks, breeding season, untransformed (=totalbrs) vs. year.

Source	SS	df	MS			
Model	298.291209	1	298.291209	Number of obs	=	13
Residual	248.631868	11	22.6028971	F (1, 11)	=	13.20
				Prob > F	=	0.0039
Total	546.923077	12	45.5769231	Rsquare	=	0.5454
				Adj Rsquare	=	0.5041
				Root MSE	=	4.7543

totalbrs	Coef.	Std. Err.	t	P>|t|	[95% Conf. Interval]	
year	1.28022	.3524085	3.633	0.004	2.055866	.504574
_cons	2554.44	699.8845	3.650	0.004	1014.004	4094.875

would be undesirable. On the other hand, if two independent variables are highly correlated, each variable could be insignificant (when controlled for the other), yet the overall model could be very significant and provide a good predictive model.

3. R^2 ("R-square") and adjusted R^2 ("Adj R-square"). The first statistic is often referred to as the coefficient of determination. While it should be familiar to all field biologists, much confusion still surrounds its use or abuse (Anderson-Sprecher 1994). The second statistic is probably unfamiliar to many, yet should be more widely known and used (Neter et al. 1990, Kleinbaum et al. 1988). R^2 can be interpreted as the proportion of variation in the dependent variable that can be accounted for by the model in question. Both statistics provide a measure of the predictive ability of a model. If R^2 and adjusted R^2 are low, this means that much variation in the Y variable is not accounted for by the model, but this does not reflect on the adequacy of the

model. In Table 5A, $R^2 = 0.637$, meaning that 36% of the variation in Black-headed Grosbeak numbers is not accounted for by an exponential decline in numbers with increasing year.

There are several drawbacks to R^2. For one, any regression model will have a positive R^2 associated with it, even a regression model that links two variables that are completely unrelated. To provide an example, we generated two random variables X, Y, integers chosen from a uniform distribution (0, 100) and which were independent of each other. Values for X were (3, 67, 98, 63, 25, 90, 34, 4, 31, 78) and for Y were (44, 91, 30, 92, 26, 56, 57, 90, 81, 47). Regressing Y on X we obtain $R^2 = 0.021$ (P = 0.69). We would feel uncomfortable in stating that "X accounted for 2.1% of the variation in Y," since in reality we know that it accounts for no such variation. The second drawback is that as one adds additional terms (additional independent variables), R^2 will always increase (Neter et al. 1990). Adjusted

R^2 (R^2a) was developed to counteract these drawbacks. Adjusted R^2 is defined as

$$R^2a = 1 - \left(\frac{n-1}{n-p}\right)\left(\frac{SSE}{SSTO}\right)$$

where n = number of observations and p = number of parameters (including the constant), SSE equals Sums of Squares of the Residual and SSTO equals Total Sums of Squares. Note that

$$R^2 = 1 - \left(\frac{SSE}{SSTO}\right)$$

In other words, R^2a is equal to R^2 after multiplying the proportion of unexplained variance by $(n-1)/(n-p)$. This ratio (the adjustment factor) is always equal to or greater than one, and therefore R^2a will always be less than or equal to R^2. As n gets large this ratio diminishes, and as p gets large, the ratio increases. The properties of R^2a are that:

1. If there is no relationship between two variables, R^2a will, on average, be equal to zero. Thus, under the null hypothesis, R^2a provides an unbiased measure of the true relationship between the two variables. In other words, if Y and X are completely unrelated, R^2a but not R^2 will, on average, equal zero. In the example cited above (of random X and Y), $R^2a = -0.101$. Any R^2a less than 0 makes it unambiguously clear that one variable does not have value in predicting the other.

2. R^2a will not necessarily increase as one adds parameters. If the gain in R^2 is small, then R^2a can decrease because the gain in R^2 does not offset the decrement due to the increase in p. Thus, R^2a can provide a good means of selecting the best predictive regression model. In fact, the model which maximizes R^2a is also the model that minimizes Mean Square Error (equivalently, Root MSE), which is a measure of residual variation about the predicted regression line.

4. Root Mean Square Error ("Root MSE"). This provides a measure of the variability about the regression line. In other words, it is the residual variation left after allowing for the effect of, in this case, year on Black-headed Grosbeak numbers. It is, literally, the square-root of the Mean Square associated with the Residual term (i.e., "error"). Root MSE would equal the standard deviation of the outcome variable if there were no explanatory power to the independent variable (i.e., $R^2 = 0.0$); otherwise, Root MSE is less than the standard

deviation. Note that Root Mean Square Error in this example is the measure of variance which the programs MONITOR and TRENDS ask for (described in detail below).

5. The regression coefficients ("Coef."), their standard errors ("Std. Err."), and results of t tests, examining whether t is significantly different from zero, are shown ("t" and "P>|t|," respectively). Shown first is the regression coefficient for the independent variable, Year. From Table 5A, our best estimate (assuming that linear regression assumptions are met) is that the number of birds observed declines at an instantaneous rate of 0.122 units, expressed in natural logarithms. This translates to an 11.5 percent decline per year, i.e., each year the number of detected birds is 0.885 times that of the previous year. When the untransformed data are analyzed (Table 5B), the best estimate is a decline of 1.28 birds per year.

Shown below the coefficient for year is the coefficient for the intercept term (here termed "constant"). The value of the intercept term provides the predicted value when the independent term (here Year) equals zero. Thus its value depends on how the independent variable is coded. Year = 0 might refer to the year 0, to the year 1900, or to any other year so designated. The designation is arbitrary and won't affect the regression coefficient for the term, Year. Note that STATA evaluates the regression coefficient for Year using a two-sided test, which we consider appropriate.

6. The 95% confidence interval for the regression coefficients are presented. We recommend that biologists examine confidence intervals for regression coefficients; a confidence interval can provide clear evidence of the precision (or lack of precision) of our analysis. For an example, where an analysis indicates no significant effect, a confidence interval may indicate that a very broad range of values is consistent with the data.

Comparing Table 5A and 5B (corresponding to Figure 1A and 1B), we see that log-transformation (Table 5A, Figure 1A) produces a better fitting model (higher R^2, more significant P-value) than does analysis of untransformed data. This implies that Black-headed Grosbeaks are declining at a, more or less, constant proportion rather than at, a more or less a constant decrease, using the absolute number of individuals. This result makes biological sense. Evaluating residuals confirms that the log-transformed model is preferable. For example, we can evaluate whether skewness and kurtosis of residuals deviates from normality for each model using the Skewness/Kurtosis test in the program STATA (StataCorp. 1999). For log-transformed data, we cannot reject the hypothesis of normality (P = 0.25), whereas for untransformed data we can reject the assumption of normality (P = 0.0003) (results obtained using "sktest" in the program STATA).

Results will not always be this clear-cut; we may want to use graphical methods to examine normality of residuals. Figure 2 shows a normal probability plot for transformed (Figure 2A) and untransformed data (Figure 2B). We won't go into the details of these plots (interested readers can refer to Kleinbaum et al. 1988, Neter et al. 1990); the main point is that if residuals are normally distributed, the data points will fall on the straight line shown. For the log-transformed data there is a reasonably good match between data points and the line; for untransformed data there is not. The graphical method does not determine whether or not the residuals are normally distributed. It does indicate to what extent transformation is or is not improving the normality of residuals.

Example 4:
Application of Simple and Multiple Regression

We now tackle a more complex example, taken from a study by the Point Reyes Bird Observatory, conducted for the California Department of Fish & Game (Nur et al. 1994). We use this example as an opportunity to provide guidance in carrying out multiple regression analysis. In July 1991 an herbicide

was accidentally spilled in and near the Sacramento River, close to Dunsmuir, CA, resulting in the death of all aquatic forms of life for a 36-mile stretch of river. In addition, terrestrial fauna and flora along the river were thought to have been impacted. Nur et al. (1994) report results of an avian monitoring project designed to assess the impact of the spill on terrestrial bird populations. A quantitative measure of presumed impact was developed by California Department of Fish & Game biologists, relying on defoliation, leaf death and other symptoms of stress exhibited by the riparian vegetation, which we term the Vegetation Damage Index. Sites along the river varied in the degree of impact, depending on the exposure to the herbicide. In general sites closer to the spill site in the downstream direction received greater damage, and therefore higher values of the damage index. Point counts were laid out in transects of 7 stations per transect, stations spaced 300 m apart, with each transect parallel to the river and 1800 m in length, with one transect per "site". All transects were in riparian habitat.

In general, there was a tendency for areas with high damage to show low species richness (Figure 3). In particular, there was an overall significant linear trend for bird species richness to decline with increasing damage, when analyzing all 55 point count stations. Output for this analysis is shown in Table 6A (using the program STATA). Note that in Table 6A, $R^2 = 0.149$, meaning that 85% of the variation in species richness among point count

Figure 2A. Normal probability plot, residuals of log-transformed data Black-headed Grosbeak

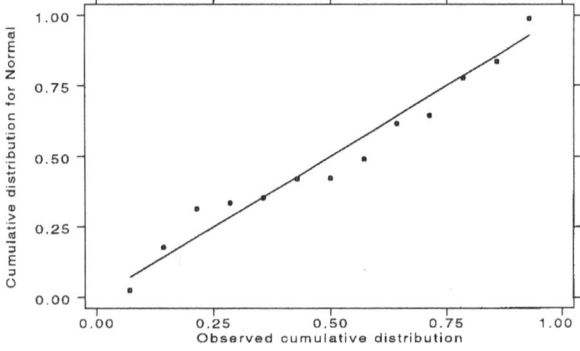

Figure 2B. Normal probability plot, residuals of untransformed data Black-headed Grosbeak

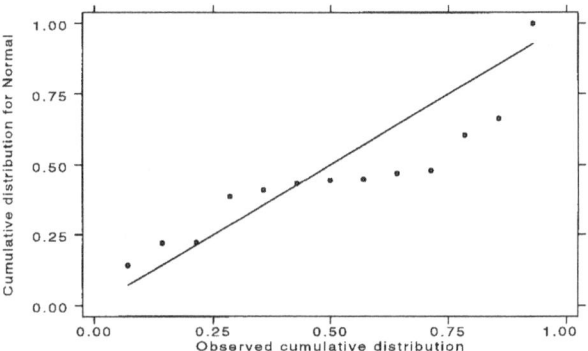

Figure 2. Evaluating the assumption of normality using graphical techniques. Comparison of "Normal probability plots" depicting residuals from analysis of log-transformed (Figure 2A) and untransformed (Figure 2B) observations of Black-headed Grosbeaks. Figure 2A and 2B depict the empirical cumulative distribution function expected if the variable were normally distributed (y-axis) vs. the observed cumulative distribution function (x-axis). If the variable in question were normally distributed then the graphed points would fall exactly on the solid line and the correlation between the two cumulative distribution functions would be +1.0. Log-transformed data conform better to a normal distribution than do untransformed observations.

---

stations is not accounted for by differences in the damage index. Our interpretation of this result is that species richness data from individual point count stations are very variable. The model is, however, highly significant, and we have no reason to think the model is inadequate.

One needs to keep in mind that there are two different objectives for which one can use regression models: (i) hypothesis testing, and (ii) prediction. In this case, a model with only vegetation damage would poorly predict species richness at a specific point count station. However, such a model achieves the objective of confirming the hypothesis that biological damage resulting from the spill was associated with diminished species richness.

Also keep in mind that the magnitude of R^2 depends on the unit of analysis. If one were to average data from several point counts and then use the averaged data in a regression analysis, this would have little effect on the P-value, yet would increase R^2 substantially. This is because some of the variation in the dependent variable has been eliminated by using mean species richness values in the regression analysis, rather then species richness at individual point count stations.

We confirmed that the linear regression analysis in Table 6A is appropriate, first by examining normality of residuals: P = 0.50, using the skewness/kurtosis test ("sktest" of STATA). In other words,

residuals do not appear to deviate from normality. We demonstrate this point graphically in Figure 4. Figure 4A shows the frequency distribution of residuals compared to a normal distribution; Figure 4B shows a quantile-normal plot for the residuals from Table 6A. (*Quartiles* and *percentiles* are examples of *quantiles*; a quantile-normal plot shows quantiles for the distribution of interest vs. quantiles from a normal distribution which matches the first distribution in terms of mean and variance.) As with a normal-probability plot (Figure 2), if the distribution is indeed normal, then the data points (quantiles in this case) would fall on the solid line shown in the Figure 4B. In this case, there seems to be a very good match, implying that residuals are approximately, normally-distributed.

That bird species richness was correlated with the Vegetation Damage Index is not by itself adequate evidence for a causal link. In a similar fashion to the analysis in Table 6A, a suite of vegetation characteristics were examined, to determine whether bird species richness, diversity and abundance were related to habitat or vegetation features. If so, such habitat variables could be confounding any relationship of the bird fauna to the impact of the spill. In one scenario, there could be no true functional relationship between bird species richness and vegetation damage, but a correlation between the two can arise if both are correlated with a vegetation feature. In another scenario, the true causal relationship between bird species richness and vegetation damage could be strong but it could be masked, wholly or in part, because both are correlated with a vegetation feature. For example, if biological damage from the spill lowered species richness, and the presence of willow (*Salix* spp.) increased species richness, then if biological damage was greatest in an area where willows were most abundant, the correlation between biological damage and bird species richness could be very weak despite a strong causal relationship between the latter two variables.

Nur et al. (1994) examined 25 habitat features to determine whether they might be correlated with abundance, species richness and/or species diversity. They found that only two habitat features were significantly correlated with abundance, species richness and diversity. The latter variables were positively correlated to the presence of willow species and negatively with the presence of big-leaf maple (*Acer macrophyllum*), i.e., the more big-leaf maple, the fewer the bird species detected. The independent variables were indices based on percent cover that was willow (on a 0 to 10 scale, corresponding to 0 to 100%), and percent cover of big-leaf maple. Results of simple linear regression of bird species richness in relation to willow cover and

Figure 3. Bird species richness in relation to Vegetation Damage Index.

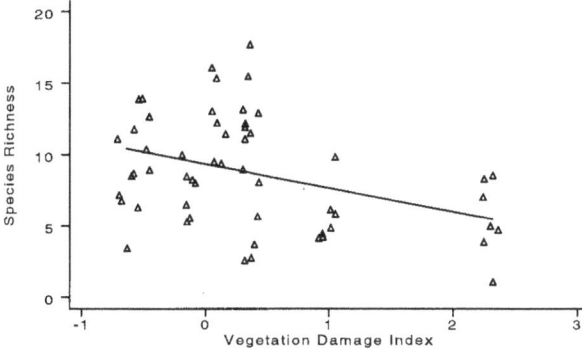

Figure 3. Bird species richness from 55 point count stations along the Sacramento River, in relation to Vegetation Damage Index. Higher values imply greater damage from spill of metam sodium (statistical results in Table 6A). Least squares line of best fit is shown. Data at each point count station have been "jittered" (Stata Corp. 1997) to reduce overlap of points.

Table 6. Sample output for linear regression analyses using STATA. See text, Example 4.

A) model: species richness [specrich] = Vegetation Damage Index [vegdindx]

Source	SS	df	MS			
Model	118.969398	1	118.969398	Number of obs	=	55
Residual	679.466965	53	12.8201314	F (1, 53)	=	9.28
Total	798.436364	54	14.7858586	Prob > F	=	0.0036
				Rsquare	=	0.1490
				Adj Rsquare	=	0.1329
				Root MSE	=	3.5805

specrich	Coef.	Std. Err.	t	P> |t|	[95% Conf. Interval]	
vegdindx	1.663229	.5459849	3.046	0.004	2.758336	.5681219
_cons	9.368597	.5243445	17.867	0.000	8.316895	10.4203

B) model: species richness [specrich] = willow cover [willotco]

Source	SS	df	MS			
Model	78.2553574	1	78.2553574	Number of obs	=	55
Residual	720.181006	53	13.5883209	F (1, 53)	=	5.76
Total	798.436364	54	14.7858586	Prob > F	=	0.0200
				Rsquare	=	0.0980
				Adj Rsquare	=	0.0810
				Root MSE	=	3.6862

specrich	Coef.	Std. Err.	t	P> |t|	[95% Conf. Interval]	
willotco	.0838145	.0349257	2.400	0.020	.0137624	.1538667
_cons	8.184659	.549244	14.902	0.000	7.083015	9.286303

C) model: species richness [specrich] = big-leaf maple Cover [bigleaco]

Source	SS	df	MS			
Model	111.19329	1	111.19329	Number of obs	=	55
Residual	687.243074	53	12.9668504	F (1, 53)	=	8.58
Total	798.436364	54	14.7858586	Prob > F	=	0.0050
				Rsquare	=	0.1393
				Adj Rsquare	=	0.1230
				Root MSE	=	3.601

specrich	Coef.	Std. Err.	t	P> |t|	[95% Conf. Interval]	
bigleaco	.0290063	.0099058	2.928	0.005	.0488740	.0091387
_cons	9.799174	.6043525	16.214	0.000	8.586997	11.01135

in relation to big-leaf maple cover are shown in Tables 6B and 6C, respectively.

The next step in the analysis was to conduct a multiple regression analysis including the three independent variables (Table 7). In this case, the primary interest was the effect of damage index while controlling for the two habitat variables. The results indicate that damage was still inversely correlated with species richness, even after controlling for one or the other habitat variable, or after controlling for both of the habitat variables (Table 7). These results give support to the view that

biological damage due to the spill reduced species richness along the river. The results do not support the alternative view that the inverse association between species richness and damage was coincidental, reflecting habitat or vegetation differences among sites along the river.

The degree and direction of differences among independent variables (if it exists) can be assessed by comparing regression coefficients in the simple regression analysis (Table 6) and in the corresponding multiple regression analysis

Figure 4A. Distribution of residuals: species richness vs. Vegetation Damage Index

Figure 4B. Quantile-quantile plot of residuals of species richness vs. Vegetation Damage Index against normal distribution

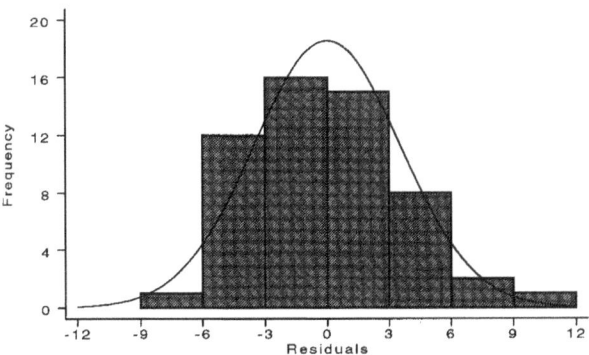

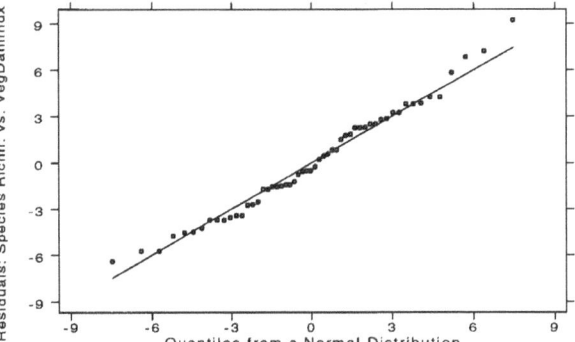

Figure 4. Evaluation of the assumption of normality of residuals using graphical techniques. Residuals of linear regression analysis of species richness are depicted (statistical model in Table 6A). Figure 4A) Frequency distribution of residuals (histogram), superimposing a frequency distribution for a normally-distributed variable with the same mean and variance as the observed variable. Figure 4B) Same residuals as in A) but graphed using a quantile-normal plot. The quantiles for the observed distribution (residuals as in Figure 4A) are plotted against the quantiles from a normally-distributed variable with the same mean and variance as the variable in question. Normality is demonstrated if the observations fall on the solid line. Both A) and B) confirm that residuals are normally distributed.

(Table 7). The effect of damage index was similar when analyzed by itself or after controlling for willow tree cover (ß = –1.66 ± 0.55 vs. ß = –1.58 ± 0.53). This indicates that willow cover did not confound the relationship between vegetation damage and species richness. On the other hand, the apparent effect of damage index, was stronger when analyzed by itself than after controlling for big-leaf maple (ß = –1.66 ± 0.55 vs. ß = –1.26 ± 0.56). Big-leaf maple tended to be more prevalent in areas where biological damage was greater (in fact, there was a significant correlation between the two, P<0.01) and thus part of the apparent reduction in species richness with increasing damage may be attributed to the influence of big-leaf maple.

Analyzing Vegetation Data in Relation to Point Count Data

In Example 4 (Tables 6-7), we provide an example of vegetation data analysis coupled with analysis of data on bird populations. In this case, the objective was to determine whether the relationship between vegetation damage and species richness was due to a direct effect of spill-induced damage, or whether the correlation was spurious and due to the fact that both were correlated with additional habitat variables. There was evidence that bird species richness was related to habitat variables (specifically the presence of willow and big-leaf maple), but these relationships could not by themselves account for the observation that bird species richness declined as vegetation damage increased.

Collecting data on many habitat and vegetation features doesn't answer the question of which habitat and vegetation features are causally related to bird abundance or distribution. If data on important variables are not collected then interpretation of the data that were collected can be compromised. There is still the problem of sifting through the data to determine which features are most closely related to the response variable in question. Many techniques have been used by investigators to evaluate multi-dimensional data, including logistic regression, discriminant analysis, principal component analysis, correspondence analysis and MANOVA (Ludwig & Reynolds 1988, Trexler & Travis 1993). It is beyond the scope of this Guide to review these various techniques; however, an example of the use of discriminant analysis is presented in the section on vegetation analysis in relation to nest-monitoring.

Design

Even if statistical inference is of no concern to the investigator, one must decide on sample size. Ralph et al. (1995) recommend at least 30 point count stations per habitat and per area of interest. If one wished to monitor two habitats in each of two areas then this would necessitate 120 point count stations. This is only a base number and the number of stations should be increased if few individuals of a species or group of species of interest are detected. Where statistical inference is a goal, then sample size will be dictated by considerations of statistical

Table 7. Analysis of point count data on Sacramento River. Relationship of bird species richness to Damage Index, controlling for vegetation/habitat characteristics (n = sample size).

A. Multiple regression analysis of bird species richness per point count station in relation to vegetation damage and willow cover

Model Statistics	Independent variable[1]	
$R^2a = 0.201$, $R^2 = 0.231$, P = 0.0011, n =55	Vegetation Damage Index	$\beta = -1.577 \pm .525$, t = -3.00, P = 0.004
	Willow cover[2]	$\beta = +0.0770 \pm .0326$, t = $+2.36$, P = 0.022

B. Multiple regression analysis of bird species richness per point-count station, in relation to vegetation damage and big-leaf maple cover.

Model Statistics	Independent variable[1]	
$R^2a = 0.186$, $R^2 = 0.216$, P = 0.0018, n = 55	Vegetation Damage Index	$\beta = -1.264 \pm .562$, t = -2.25, P = 0.029
	Big-leaf maple cover[2]	$\beta = -0.0213 \pm .0102$, t = -2.10, P = 0.041

C. Multiple regression analysis of bird species richness per point-count station, in relation to vegetation damage, willow cover, and big-leaf maple cover

Model Statistics	Independent variable[3]	
$R^2a = 0.229$, $R^2 = 0.272$, P = 0.0010, n = 55	Vegetation Damage Index	$\beta = -1.273 \pm .547$, t = -2.33, P = 0.024
	Willow cover[2]	$\beta = +0.0651 \pm .0329$, t = $+1.98$, P = 0.053
	Big-leaf maple cover[2]	$\beta = -0.0170 \pm .0101$, t = -1.68, P = 0.100

[1] Both considered simultaneously
[2] On 0 – 10 scale
[3] All three considered simultaneously

power; examples include comparisons among treatments and monitoring programs that assess temporal trends (Gerrodette 1987, 1991, Link & Hatfield 1990; for a general review, see Thomas & Krebs 1997).

Dawson (1981) has derived an equation for determining the sample size, in this case the number of point count stations necessary to detect an effect of interest with 50% power. He assumed that each station is surveyed once, and that the number of detections (for each species or group of species) at each station follows a Poisson distribution. If the distribution of bird-detections deviates from Poisson distribution, then the formula would need to be revised. Under a Poisson distribution the mean number of detections and the variance in the number of detections per point count station would be equal. If the variance substantially exceeds the mean, or vice versa, one could either modify his formula, or use other formulas (as modified below).

Dawson also assumed that there were two groups (two habitats, two treatments, etc.) of interest. The formula for sample size calculations is

$$n > \frac{(3.84)(20000)}{(d^2)(m)} \qquad [1]$$

where m = average number of detections per sampling unit and d = percent difference between group 1 and group 2, defined as

$$d = (100)\left(\frac{m_1 - m_2}{m}\right)$$

For example, if $m_1 = 2.5$ and $m_2 = 1.5$, then m = 2.0 and d = 50.

Thus, where the average number of individuals detected per station is equal to 1, the number of stations per group necessary to achieve 50% power to detect a 50% difference in mean abundance is 30.7. To detect a 25% difference would require 123 point count stations per group. That is, to detect half the difference (all else being equal) requires 4 times the sample size! This exemplifies a general rule—precision increases, and therefore standard errors decrease, in proportion to the square root of sample size. Note that as average number of detections increases, sample size (number of stations) decreases linearly—and proportionally. This emphasizes that calculations of necessary sample sizes reflect the average number of detections. Thus, if the average number of individuals detected per station is 0.5 rather than

1.0, then twice as many point count stations are required, i.e., 246 and 61.4 point count stations would be required per group to detect a 25% and 50% difference, respectively.

As stated earlier, it is common practice to use a higher level of statistical power (e.g., 80%) in designing studies. Dawson (1981) only considered 50% power, but his results can be extended to consider more stringent levels of power as follows.

For other levels of power substitute the following (approximate) values for the 3.84 in Equation 1: for 70% power, substitute 6.15; for 80% power substitute 7.84; for 90% power substitute 10.50.

These values were derived from a more general formula for comparison of means using two-sample t tests, i.e.,

$$n = \frac{(\sigma_1^2 + \sigma_2^2)\,(z_{1-\alpha/2} + z_{1-\beta})^2}{(\mu_1 - \mu_2)^2} \qquad [2]$$

where n is the required sample size for each sample, σ_1^2 refers to variance in sample 1, etc., μ_1 refers to mean value in sample 1, etc., and $z_{subscript}$ is a "normal deviate" (also called z-score). For example, for $\alpha = 0.05$, $z_{(1-\alpha/2)} = z_{0.975} = 1.96$; for power = 0.8, $z_{0.8} = 0.84$; for power = 0.5, $z_{0.5} = 0.0$; for power = 0.9, $z_{0.9} = 1.28$; and so on (Snedecor & Cochran 1989). The experimenter would set the difference between means; σ_1 and σ_2 are fixed by the investigator (i.e., determined independently). For a Poisson-distributed variable, $\mu_1 = \sigma_1^2$ and $\mu_2 = \sigma_2^2$.

Thus, with 1 individual detected on average per point count station, approximately 250 and 63 point count stations would be required per group to achieve 80% power to detect between-group differences of 25% and 50%, respectively. With 0.5 individual detected per point count, at least double these sample sizes (500 and 126) would be required per group to achieve the same 80% power. Note that the minimum recommendation of Ralph et al. (1995), i.e., 30 point count stations per habitat or treatment, provides 80% power to detect a 50% difference given an average of 2.0 detections per station, but only yields 50% power to detect a 50% difference given 1.0 detections per station.

Where there are three or more groups of interest, we recommend the same number of point count stations per group be maintained. Thus to detect a 50% between-group difference with 50% power and 0.5 individual detected, on average, per station, one would need either 123 point count stations (total) allocated among 2 groups or 184 point count stations

for 3 groups. This is admittedly a conservative approach. It would maintain the same degree of precision per group, whether or not there are two or more groups.

Buckland et al. (1993) present a formula for calculating sample size (number of point count stations) necessary to achieve a specified precision in estimating population size. They assume that one has conducted a pilot study of k_0 stations and detected a total of n_0 individuals (assuming no aggregations or clustering of individuals, as is the case in flocks). Their formula for number of stations, K, is

$$K = \left(\frac{b}{[CV(D)]^2}\right)\left(\frac{k_0}{n_0}\right)$$

where CV(D) is the coefficient of variation of abundance, i.e., the standard error (not the standard deviation) of abundance divided by mean abundance. For example if one wished to estimate abundance such that the standard error was 20% of the mean value, then CV(D) = 0.2. b is a factor that depends on several variables and can be estimated from pilot data (Buckland et al 1993); however, they state that it will usually be about 3. Thus if 15 individuals are detected at 10 point count stations on the pilot study, CV(D) = 0.2 (by design) and b = 3, then K = $^{3.0}/_{0.04} \times 0.667 = 50$ point count stations. This will be sufficient to establish a confidence interval for abundance that ranges ± 40% of the true value.

Power and Sample Size Analysis Using TRENDS

Recently, there has been a veritable explosion of software now available for determination of power and/or necessary sample size to achieve specified power (Thomas & Krebs 1997, available on the world-wide web at http://www.interchg.ubc.ca/cacb/power/review/). Two specialized, free programs are available for monitoring programs that evaluate trends, whether those trends are temporal or spatial.

For analysis of trend data using linear regression, a user-friendly program, TRENDS (Gerrodette 1987, 1991), has been written by Tim Gerrodette and is available, free of charge, from the Internet (ftp://ftp.im.nbs.gov/pub/software/CSE/wsb21515/trends.zip; also available from T. Gerrodette, Southwest Fisheries Science Center, P.O. Box 271, La Jolla, CA 92038, in which case please provide him a 3.5″ IBM-compatible floppy disk). A User's Guide is provided with the software. We offer the following as guidance in using and interpreting results from TRENDS.

TRENDS can be used for either temporal trends or spatial trends, with regard to changes in abundance. The program TRENDS can compute any one of the following parameters:

1. Number of samples (either number of occasions, for temporal trends, or number of sites for spatial trends) (n);

2. Rate of change (expressed as proportional decline or increase of the total population, e.g., –0.10 refers to 10% decline per unit of time or space; 0.05 refers to 5% growth per unit of time or space, etc.) (r);

3. Measure of variation about the trend line, which Gerrodette (1989) refers to as "initial coefficient of variation" (CV1);

4. Significance level (α);

5. Power (1-ß, where ß is the probability of making a Type II error).

If four of these parameters are specified, the fifth parameter is strictly determined, and its value can be calculated by TRENDS. For example, if one specifies number of samples, magnitude of the rate of change, the variation about the trend line, and the a level, TRENDS calculates power. In the same way one can calculate the necessary number of temporal or spatial samples to achieve a specified power to detect an effect of specified magnitude.

If one is evaluating temporal trends, then the *number of samples* refers to the number of sampling occasions—most commonly the number of years studied. If several surveys or point counts contribute to a single year's data, these would be averaged together to yield a single datum for that year. In the program TRENDS, if 10 point counts are conducted in each of 10 years, the number of samples is 10, not 100.

The measure of variation about the trend line is given as the coefficient of variation (= standard deviation [or standard error] divided by the mean), symbolized in the program as CV1. CV1 is inversely related to precision. Gerrodette refers to CV1 as "initial coefficient of variation", which is misleading. The best way to obtain an estimate of CV1 is to use data from a trend analysis to determine root mean square error (Table 5) and then divide this by the mean (or expected value). Gerrodette provides an example where CV1 was estimated from replicate counts on the same population in the same year which was the initial year of the study. We strongly advise against this practice because doing so estimates only the part of the variation due to measurement error. An additional part of the

variation about the trend line is due to stochastic variation in abundance, which also needs to be incorporated into CV1.

The other three parameters are straight forward. In addition, TRENDS requires one to make additional specifications:

6. Whether to use a 1- or 2-tailed test,

7. Whether population change is linear or exponential,

8. Whether one's test statistic is the z or t statistic, and

9. How CV1 is related to abundance.

Although the first three are straight-forward, we do have some recommendations. First, a 2-tailed test is almost always the appropriate test, because the possibility of an increase in population cannot be ruled out, and would be of interest just as much as a decline in population. Secondly, for temporal trends, exponential growth is to be preferred. Exponential growth implies that the growth or decline is a constant percentage, e.g., a population increases at 10% per year. Furthermore, this assumption is in accord with the definition of r, the rate of change. Thirdly, if one is estimating CV1 from data, then the t statistic is appropriate (Link & Hatfield 1990).

The relationship of CV1 to abundance is complex. TRENDS assumes that variance (VAR) in a population estimate is (i) proportional to abundance (A), (ii) proportional to A^2, or (iii) proportional to A^3. TRENDS does not allow for VAR to be independent of abundance, or for VAR to be inversely proportional to abundance. Noting that mean abundance is proportional to abundance and that the CV is the square-root of VAR divided by the mean, options (i) to (iii) imply that:

(i)   CV is proportional to $1/\sqrt{A}$,

(ii)   CV is independent of A, or

(iii)   CV is proportional to $\sqrt{A}$.

TRENDS allows one to choose among these three options. Which option one chooses will affect calculated power, necessary sample sizes, etc. (Link & Hatfield 1990). As guidance for choosing among the options, Gerrodette (1987) offers the following: for quadrats, strip transects, line transects, or catch per unit effort (CPUE), CV is proportional to $1/\sqrt{A}$. For distance sampling, CV is independent of A. For the single mark-recapture using the Peterson method, CV is proportional to

√A. Presumably, option (i) applies to standard (fixed-distance) point count data, since a point count can be thought of as a line transect of length zero (Buckland et al. 1993).

Example 5:
Power Calculation Using TRENDS

To provide an example of one of the uses of TRENDS, we consider surveys of Black-headed Grosbeaks (based on data given in Example 3 and Figure 1). CV1 for a single annual count (of log-transformed data) is estimated to be 0.284 (root mean square error [see Table 5A] divided by mean value). Assuming $\alpha=0.05$, exponential population change (i.e., constant percentage change each year), a 2-tailed test, use of the t-statistic, and CV1 proportional to $1/\sqrt{A}$, the probability (power) to detect a 5% decline per year after 10 years is 34%. If, instead, CV1 is independent of A, then the power to detect a 5% decline per year after 10 years is 29%. It is difficult to say whether option (i) or option (ii) is more appropriate, but the difference between the two estimates is small. Thus, the power to detect a substantial decline (amounting to 40% decline after 10 years) is fairly weak. If we increase the time scale to 15 years, however, power increases to 89% (under option i). Under this scenario we would have appreciable power to detect a decline, but after 15 years the population will have declined by 54%. An alternative means of increasing power would be to increase the precision of our annual estimate, which implies lowering the variance about the trend line, i.e., decreasing CV1. If CV1 could be lowered from 0.284 to 0.200, power would increase (assuming 5% decline over a 10 year period) from 34% to 59%. CV1 might be lowered if sources of error could be reduced (e.g., conduct surveys at the same time of year) or if replicate surveys were carried out and the results for each year then averaged.

One can easily use TRENDS to determine, instead, the minimum number of years required to attain 80% power to detect a 5% decline per year (14 years, assuming option i).

Using MONITOR

Whereas TRENDS uses an analytic approach to determine sample size, power, etc., MONITOR (developed by James Gibbs) uses computer simulation. Link & Hatfield (1990) argue that computer simulation is to be preferred to analytic solutions, because the latter can only provide approximate results. The program MONITOR is easy to use (ftp://ftp.im.nbs.gov/pub/software/monitor), and a Manual is readily available as well. Users of the program should take into account the following points.

1. Similar to TRENDS, only one data point per plot (or transect or route) is allowed per time unit (e.g., per year). Unlike TRENDS, MONITOR can allow for analyses conducted on several plots at once. Where several plots (transects, routes, etc.) are analyzed at once, MONITOR calculates a weighted trend (see below for further discussion of weighting).

2. Whereas "plots", can refer to "routes" or "transects," it can also refer to individual point count stations if they will be analyzed in this way (and not simply pooled across a transect or route). The maximum number of "plots" is 250.

3. When several surveys are conducted for each plot in the same year (or breeding season or other interval of interest), MONITOR averages across these data (i.e., collapsing the data into a single data point per plot per year).

4. A critical variable is "variance of plot counts." This variance is used to simulate variation about the specified trend line. The manual suggests that within-year variation (determined from multiple surveys) can be used to estimate between-year variance, but this will generally not be valid. The correct estimate is the variance about the trend line, just as with TRENDS.

5. As with TRENDS, the trend can be linear or exponential. We strongly recommend an exponential trend for reasons discussed above, unless data at hand indicate a linear trend is more appropriate.

6. Data from multiple plots can be weighted according to mean abundance, but variance about the plot-specific trends is not used in weighting. This is less than satisfactory, because it means that a poorly-estimated trend has as much weight as a well-estimated trend.

7. When data are collected from several plots, MONITOR de-means the values (subtracting off the mean value for each plot) before calculating the variance. Otherwise, variance due to habitat differences among plots will be included in the estimate of sampling variance (which we are interested in). However, this de-meaning is undesirable because it over-corrects. That is, suppose we have n plots that are true replicates. In this case, all between-plot differences are due to sampling variation, which will have been completely removed by de-meaning. A better approach would be to use a covariate (or set of covariates) to characterize habitat variation, and then use residuals from a regression on the habitat covariate, to provide an appropriate measure of variance.

Power and Sample-Size Analyses: Other Sources

Several stand-alone statistical packages are now available that can calculate power for a variety of statistical tests and situations (reviewed by Thomas & Krebs 1997). In their review, Thomas and Krebs mention five programs that they could recommend. Of these we highlight two: the first is PASS (Power And Sample Size; available from NCSS Statistical Software, 329 North 1000 East, Kaysville, UT 84037; http://www.ncss.com/pass.html). When a class of ecology graduate students was asked to compare PASS with three other recommendable power and sample size programs, 17 out of 19 students preferred PASS! It is flexible, accurate, easy to use, and easy to learn. The cost is moderate ($249). The other program we mention (also reviewed by Thomas and Krebs) is GPOWER (Erdfelder et al. 1996); though this program did not score as highly as PASS, it is free (http://www.psychologie.uni-trier.de:8000/projects/gpower.html). Thomas and Krebs (1997) examined several general-purpose statistical programs with built-in power analyses, but found none that they could recommend.

Two other valuable sources for power analysis are on the web. The Patuxent Wildlife Research Center of USGS has an excellent page, that includes a power analysis program for calculating power for monitoring programs, using the data in a manner similar to TRENDS. This is available at http://www.im.nbs.gov/powcase/powcase.html. Also available is a web page dedicated to the discussion and calculation of power analyses at http://www.im.nbs.gov/powcase/powlinks.html. This site has both MONITOR and TRENDS available as freeware.

A number of statistical texts treat the problem of determining power. Fleiss (1981) provides an excellent practical treatment of the problem when the outcome is binary (only one of two outcomes), or can be expressed as a rate or proportion. Thus, his text can be very useful for studies of survival or studies in which the outcome is presence or absence. Cohen (1988) gives an extensive non-technical treatment of power analysis for ANOVA.

III. Demographic Monitoring: Mist-nets

Mist-nets can be used to provide estimates of many parameters: 1. relative abundance, 2. species composition (richness, diversity), 3. productivity, as measured by production or abundance of HY (Hatching Year) birds, and 4. annual adult survival. In addition, one can, in theory, estimate 5. offspring survivorship to breeding age using data from mist-nets but this is an area that is only now being investigated by researchers. Regarding abundance and species composition, methods of analysis are the same as described for analysis of point count data. Recent examples of analyses of trends in abundance include Johnson & Geupel (1996) and Chase et al. (1997); Silkey et al. (1999) discuss the validity of inferring population trends from mist-net capture data. Nur et al. (1994) analyzed patterns of abundance along the upper Sacramento River (Example 4) using mist-net capture data and using point-count data. Mist nets cannot, however, provide an absolute measure of abundance. On the other hand, they can provide an age-specific, and sometimes sex-specific, measure of abundance, with a resolution that cannot be matched by point-count or line-transect data.

Analysis of Productivity

The number of HY birds caught in a standardized mist-netting study can provide an index of production of young (DeSante & Geupel 1987, Nur & Geupel 1993b, DeSante et al. 1993). Such data have been analyzed in three ways: (i) analysis of total number of HY birds caught; (ii) analysis of number of HY birds caught per AHY (After Hatching Year, i.e., adult) caught; or (iii) analysis of per cent of all birds who are HY. Among these parameters, (iii) is just a transformation of (ii), and vice versa, provided that all birds are classified as HY or AHY (total = AHY + HY). This can be seen as follows: let HY/AHY=R. Then proportion of all birds that are HY = HY/(AHY + HY), can be written as

$$\text{proportion HY} = \frac{1}{1 + (\frac{1}{R})}$$

Thus, (iii) only re-expresses (ii), but the interpretation of (ii) is more direct: the number of fledged young per adult.

Nur & Geupel (1993a, 1993b) point out that there are hazards with including the number of AHY birds caught as a measure of productivity (as do indices ii and iii above): notably, the catchment area of HY and AHY can differ markedly (Nur & Geupel 1993a). Secondly, many AHY birds are transient, i.e., not breeding locally. As an alternative, one can use the measure in (i), HY birds alone. If one finds differences in the number of HY birds caught in two sets of sites, or can establish a trend in HY numbers, this provides information about the production of young on a *population level*, but it may or may not indicate differences or trends in productivity *per pair*. Thus we recommend that, if variations in breeding population size can safely be ruled out, in comparing areas or comparing years, the number of HY be analyzed by itself (see examples in Nur & Geupel 1993b). Otherwise, the biologist should analyze (ii) or (iii). Example 6 demonstrates different ways of analyzing productivity.

Example 6:
Analyses of Productivity.

This example is taken from the study of the impact of the herbicide metam sodium on landbird populations of the Sacramento River, described in Example 4. Table 8 shows a species-by-species analysis of productivity as measured in two ways, HY birds per 100 net-hours, and proportion of HY birds in the catch.

To examine patterns of productivity we selected those species with sufficient sample size. Our criteria were: (1) at least 36 individuals caught (of all age classes) from the 9 sites, and (2) at least 12 HY individuals caught, total, from the 9 sites. Six species met both criteria (Table 8). The "36 individual criterion" implied that each site averaged 4 or more individuals caught, which we considered a minimal acceptable number. We would have preferred to impose a minimum of 45 individuals (i.e., 5 individuals caught per site on average), but then we would have had fewer than 6 species to analyze. The second criterion, at least 12 HY individuals caught among the 9 sites, may seem too low a threshold (an average of 1.33 HY individuals caught per site). Nevertheless, we wished to include possible instances where reproductive success was poor or nil at a number of the 9 sites; such apparent reproductive failure might be especially informative. Thus, a hypothetical species with 5, 4, 2, 1, 0, 0, 0, 0, 0 captures at 9 sites would qualify with respect to the "12 HY" criterion. On the other hand, a species with 12 HY captures at 1 site, and 8 sites without any HY captures is not particularly informative. We thus set a 3rd criterion: HY captures at a minimum of 3 sites. All species that met criteria (1) and (2), also met the 3rd criterion.

To analyze the HY capture data, we log-transformed capture rates (birds caught per 100 net-hours), for each species at each site. To avoid taking the log of 0 (which is undefined), we added a constant—in this case, 1—before log-transforming. Had there been no zeroes in the data set, we would not have added any constant; there would have been no need to. Whereas adding a constant before log-transformation is standard practice, it can lead to bias (Thomas 1996). However, the direction of bias is conservative: adding a constant makes it somewhat more difficult to detect an effect (e.g., to detect a trend). We recommend that investigators try two different constants (e.g., adding 0.5 and adding 1) and determine if results are similar. If they are, then the investigator has some confidence that his or her results are not unduly sensitive to the chosen constant.

For analysis of the proportion of HY in the catch, we used the logit-transformation. In the case where total captures = HY + AHY,

$$\text{logit(proportion of HY)} = \log_e(\text{HY/AHY}).$$

Table 8. Analysis of mist-net captures, Sacramento River 1993: Relationship to Damage Index for the six species with adequate sample size (at least 12 HY individuals caught, and at least 36 individuals, total, caught, among 9 sites).

A) Dependent Variable: Hatching Year birds per 100 net hours[a]

Species	Analysis	Number HY Caught
Black-headed Grosbeak	ß = −0.369 ± 0.192, P = 0.096, R^2a= 0.251, R^2= 0.345	12
McGillivray's Warbler	ß = −0.519 ± 0.405, P = 0.240, R^2a= 0.074, R^2= 0.190	39
Orange-crowned Warbler	ß = −0.226 ± 0.078, P = 0.023, R^2a= 0.479, R^2= 0.544	15
Song Sparrow	ß = −0.565 ± 0.357, P = 0.16, R^2a= 0.159, R^2= 0.264	55
Spotted Towhee	ß = −0.649 ± 0.227, P = 0.024, R^2a= 0.472, R^2= 0.538	32
Yellow-breasted Chat	ß = −0.462 ± 0.169, P = 0.029, R^2a= 0.449, R^2= 0.518	13

B) Dependent Variable: Proportion of Hatching Year birds[b]

Species	Analysis	Number of Sites
Black headed Grosbeak	ß = −0.901 ± 0.566, P = 0.15, R^2a= 0.161, R^2= 0.266	9
McGillivray's Warbler	ß = −1.054 ± 1.115, P > 0.3, R^2a= 0.006, R^2= 0.130	9
Orange-crowned Warbler	ß = +1.623 ± 0.432, P = 0.007, R^2a= 0.622, R^2= 0.669	9
Song Sparrow	ß = −0.819 ± 0.690, P > 0.2, R^2a= 0.170, R^2= 0.274	9
Spotted Towhee	ß = −1.707 ± 0.789, P = 0.074, R^2a= 0.344, R^2= 0.438	8
Yellow-breasted Chat	ß = −1.497 ± 1.117, P > 0.2, R^2a= 0.117, R^2= 0.264	7

[a] Hatching Year Birds caught per 100 net-hours, log-transformed, i.e. ln((HY caught + 1)/100 net-hours). Results of simple regression analyses for effect of Vegetation Damage Index. Sample size = 9 sites for each analysis.
[b] Proportion of Hatching Year birds, logit-transformed Results of simple regression analyses for effect of Vegetation Damage Index. Sample size (number of sites) for each analysis is shown.

Table 9. Analysis of mist-net captures, Sacramento River, 1993: Relationship of HY, and proportion HY birds caught in relation to Vegetation Damage Index. Results of simple regression analyses; independent variable in each model is Vegetation Damage Index. Number of sites (sample size) is 9. Capture rates have been log-transformed, i.e. ln((number of birds + 1)/100 net-hours).

Dependent Variable	Analysis
HY birds/100 net-hours	ß = −0.795 ± 0.201, P = 0.006, R^2a= 0.646, R^2= 0.690
Proportion of HY birds caught logit-transformed	ß = −0.360 ± 0.120, P = 0.028, R^2a= 0.453, R^2= 0.521

The logit transformation is a commonly used transformation in biological analysis and forms the basis of logistic regression (Chapter V). Note that the logit(proportion of HY) is undefined when the denominator (in this case number AHY caught) is zero. We could have added a constant to the denominator to avoid this "problem" but did not; we consider it biologically appropriate that our measure of productivity is undefined when there are (apparently) no adults present. For the analysis in Table 8B, sites could not be included where logit(proportion of HY) was undefined, i.e., where no AHY were caught. This applied to two of the six species.

As shown in Table 8, of the six species analyzed, three showed a significant decline in capture rate with increasing biological damage. Analyses of the HY/AHY ratio indicated a consistently downward trend with increasing damage (5 out of 6 species had a negative slope), but no species had a significant negative trend. These results suggest that sample sizes of individual species were likely too small to reveal significant patterns, and a pooled analysis was carried out, shown in Table 9. Analyses of all HY and AHY caught for all terrestrial bird species were pooled and the results confirmed a significant decrease in productivity with increase in damage symptoms.

Analysis of Adult Survival

Survival can be analyzed in two ways: using capture/recapture methods or analyzing "return rate". Return rate is the proportion of individuals observed in one time period (we refer to this period as t), which are observed again (resighted, recaptured, etc.) in the following time period (period $t + 1$). Thus return rate is the product of two processes: survival from period t to period $t + 1$, and resighting (or recapture) in period $t + 1$. Resighting probability is defined as the probability an individual is resighted at time $t + 1$, given that an individual has survived until time $t + 1$ (Clobert et al. 1987, Nur & Clobert 1988). In short,

$$return\ rate = \frac{survival}{probability} \times \frac{recapture}{probability}.$$

(We use "recapture" in a broad sense to refer to both resighting and recapture.) The justification for analyzing return rate as a means of studying survival is the assumption that recapture probability is 100% or, at least, that it can be treated as a constant. This assumption is likely to be violated when one is comparing the sexes, or comparing different species or even different populations. Capture/recapture methodology analyzes both parameters, survival and recapture probability.

In this way, survival can be estimated independently of recapture probability and one can test for differences in survival as well as differences in recapture probability (Lebreton et al. 1992). It would seem that capture/recapture methodology provides a superior means to analyze survival and, in theory, it does. However, there are three drawbacks to its usage:

1. Capture/recapture methods require at least three field seasons to estimate survival for one year, instead of two. 2. More data are required to carry out these analyses than with return-rate analyses, because two parameters are being estimated instead of one. 3. The optimal software for survival analyses is not yet available, one that combines flexibility, statistical power, and ease of use, without requiring specialized instruction. In the meantime, there are several programs available which can fill the gap (for more detailed discussion, see Lebreton et al. 1993). Table 10 summarizes statistical programs that are available for analyzing capture/recapture data (based on Lebreton et al. 1992). Below we discuss six programs that have been widely used (SURGE, RELEASE, MARK, SURPH, JOLLY, and JOLLYAGE).

General Comments. Capture/recapture models such as SURGE require at least three field seasons (usually years) in order to estimate survival between the first season and the second, though it is possible, making some assumptions, to derive survival estimates for the period between the second and third field seasons. Thus ten field seasons would yield estimates of survival for each of eight years, and so on. It is strongly recommended that the capture occasions be equally spaced and generally speaking the programs SURGE, RELEASE, JOLLY, and JOLLYAGE assume this. If one is seeking to estimate annual survival, then the capture "occasion" is the year or breeding season. In each year, an individual is either caught or re-sighted (scored a "1"), or not observed (scored a "0"). This allows one to construct a capture history for each individual (a string of 1's and 0's). The capture history data set consists of rows of individual capture histories. The capture occasions could instead be defined time periods within a single year. This would allow one to estimate survival within a year. In most survival analyses of constant-effort mist-netting data (Peach 1993, Chase et al. 1997), all captures for each species from a single breeding season have been pooled.

SURGE. This program is available from AVENIX (14, Avenue de Montpellier, 34680 SAINT-GEORGES-D'ORQUES, France; fax number (33) 67 40 22 90. The program comes with a user's manual (Pradel & Lebreton 1993), and runs on

Table 10. Evaluation and summary of available computer program software used for the analysis of animal marking and surveying studies. Presence of an attribute = "+", absence of an attribute = "–"; other symbols explained below. Based on Table 9 in Lebreton et al. (1992).

Program Name	Key Reference	U	G	C	O	M	P	L	R	W	T	V	D
SURGE	Lebreton et al. 1992	+	+	P	B	M	O	S	B	–	+	+	+
RELEASE	Burnham et al. 1987	+	+	P	B	M	O	S	B	+	+	+	–
JOLLY/JOLLYAGE	Pollack et al. 1990	+	+	P	B	S	O	B	L	–	–	–	–
SURVIV	White 1986	–	–	B	B	M	O	S	B	+	+	+	+
POPAN3	Arnason & Schwartz 1986	+	+	M	O	S	B	B	L	–	–	+	–
RECAPCO	Buckland 1980	–	–	B	S	S	O	B	B	–	–	–	–
CAPTURE	White et al. 1982	+	+	B	B	S	C	N	L	–	–	–	–
CONTRAST	Sauer & Williams 1989	+	–	P	B	–	–	–	B	–	–	–	–
BROWNIE/ESTIMATE	Brownie et al. 1985	+	+	B	B	M	O	S	R	–	–	–	–

U = easy to use, with good documentation and/or interactive input

G = For general use, available without cost or low cost

C = Available for PC = "P", mainframe = "M" computers or "B" = both

O = "O"= object code, "S" = source code, "B"= both

M = "M"= Multiple or "S"= single data sets

P = "O"= open and "C"= closed populations models, "B"= both

L = "N"= population numbers, "S"= survival rates, "B"= both

R = "R"= recovery data, "L'= live recapture, "B"= both

W = Power computation

T = Treatment/control experiments

V = Covariates

D = User-defined model allowed

IBM-compatible PC's. SURGE is also available by anonymous ftp at: ftp://ftp.cefe.cnrs-mop.fr/. SURGE is very flexible and statistically powerful. It can be difficult to use, especially for the unsophisticated user, even with the manual at hand. Fortunately, a detailed User's Guide ("A Practical Guide to Capture-Recapture Analysis Using SURGE") has been published (Cooch et al. 1996), oriented towards the intermediate user. This document is available at a cost of US $20 (postage and shipping included) from Evan Cooch (Dept. Biological Science, Simon Fraser Univ., Burnaby, BC, V5A 1S6, CANADA) and from the senior author of this document. Chapters can be downloaded from http://www.biol.sfu.ca/cmr/surge. The Practical Guide also provides a concise introduction to using and interpreting RELEASE.

For discussion of SURGE, its rationale, capabilities, etc., the reader is referred to Clobert et al. (1987), Nur & Clobert (1988) and Lebreton et al. (1992). Good examples of the use of SURGE are provided by Peach et al. (1991), Peach (1993), and Chase et al. (1997). SURGE allows one to use and test models in which recapture and survival

probability vary from year to year, site to site, or in some other way due to some characteristic of the individual, including age of the individual. Thus, one can, for example, test whether recapture probability or survival probability varies from site to site; if so, one should incorporate such variation in any further analyses. The independent variable can be quantitative or categorical. If one concludes that recapture or survival probability does not vary with year, site, etc., then such variation can be dropped from the statistical model and further analyses can use the more parsimonious model (Lebreton et al. 1992).

Another example of a type of analysis that can be carried out with SURGE concerns sex-differences. For example, one can examine whether survival varies with sex, whether it varies with time (e.g., testing for a linear trend in survival), and one can also examine whether temporal trends in survival are similar or different for the two sexes. Another example of an analysis possible with SURGE is to examine whether survival or recapture probability is density-dependent (Cooch et al. 1996).

Example 7:
Recapture Probability and Territory Status

The following example is taken from Nur & Geupel (1993a). Survival of Wrentits (*Chamaea fasciata*), a highly sedentary species, caught in standardized mist-netting at the Palomarin field station, was assessed over an 11 year period (1980 to 1991). There was no significant year-to-year variation in survival probability or recapture probability. Survival and recapture probabilities were analyzed for two different classes of individuals: (1) known territory holders and (2) individuals not holding territories (floaters). Additional data indicated that most floaters were very transient. The results of the SURGE analysis are shown in Table 11 for the two classes of individuals (territory holders and floaters) and for all individuals, pooled. The results indicate the value of distinguishing individuals with high site fidelity (territory holders) from transient individuals. Survival of territory holders was estimated to be 57%. But when territory holders and floaters were pooled, the survival estimate was much lower at 31%. The reason was that recapture probability was very different for the two groups: 71% for territory holders and 5% for floaters. When these two groups were pooled, thus violating the assumption of equal survival and recapture probability among individuals, the result was a poor estimate of recapture probability and thus an unreliable estimate of survival.

The other programs: RELEASE, MARK, JOLLY, and JOLLYAGE, are freely available to the public (RELEASE and MARK: G.C. White, Dept of Fishery & Wildlife Biology, Colorado State Univ., Fort Collins, CO 80523; JOLLY and JOLLYAGE: J.E. Hines, Patuxent Wildlife Research Center, Laurel, MD 20708).

RELEASE. The program is described in Burnham et al. (1987). The program itself is fairly easy to use. It can estimate and compare survival among groups as well as conduct goodness-of-fit tests to determine if assumptions of analyses are being met (e.g., there is no heterogeneity in capture probability among individuals, there is no recapture-avoidance). A major drawback is that no easy to use manual is available. Those who wish to use RELEASE to conduct goodness-of-fit tests are urged to consult the Practical Guide to SURGE (Cooch et al. 1996) where RELEASE is treated in the Appendix.

MARK. This program is in final-development stage. A beta-test version is available from http://www.cnr.colostate.edu/~gwhite/mark/mark.htm. No User's Manual as such is available but documentation is available from the same source. This program is menu-driven and provides an excellent combination of flexibility, power, and ease-of-use. One disadvantage of MARK is that it is designed only to run on Windows95. Novices in capture/recapture analysis are recommended to consult the Practical Guide to SURGE (Cooch et al. 1996), where much of the rationale and background material for this body of analysis is presented.

SURPH (SURvival under Proportional Hazards). This program can be used to analyze survival rates, using both capture-recapture data, and using known fate data (also called time to death or time to failure data). SURPH has been developed by Steven G. Smith, John R. Skalski and others. For more information, direct enquiries to surph@cqs.washington.edu; also see the web site: http://www.cqs.washington.edu/surph/index.html. An extensive, informative, and easy to use manual is available. In general, the program is easy to use and flexible. One of its greatest strengths is that, unlike other capture-recapture programs discussed, it allows one to analyze the effects of individual-level covariates on survival and recapture probability. Body mass of adults at the time of first capture or date of fledging are two possible examples of individual level covariates.

JOLLY and JOLLYAGE. These programs are described in Pollock et al. (1990). These two programs are the least sophisticated of those discussed. The main features to recommend them

Table 11. Results of SURGE analysis of Wrentits, by territory status.

	Survival Probability		Recapture Probability	
	Per cent	95% C.I.	Per cent	95% C.I.
Territory holders	57[a]	47-67	71[b]	53-84
Non-territory holders (floaters)	38[a]	13-72	5[b]	1-18
All adults, pooled	31	22-41	38	23-56

[a] Difference in parameter estimates, territory holders vs. floaters: P > 0.3
[b] Difference in parameter estimates, territory holders vs. floaters: P < 0.0001

are that they are easy to obtain, easy to use, and the manual for their use (Pollock et al. 1990) is relatively easy to follow. One advantage of these two programs is that, unlike the above-discussed programs, JOLLY and JOLLYAGE also estimate population size.

JOLLY assumes no age differentiation (i.e., all ages have similar survival and recapture probability); JOLLYAGE allows for two age-classes. (In contrast, there is no limitation to the number of age classes considered in SURGE.) JOLLY allows a choice between one of five models (Table 12). In model A, survival (symbolized phi) and recapture probability (symbolized p) are both time-specific (e.g., they vary from year to year). Model A' is like model A but it allows for deaths only, and no new recruitment, whether by birth or by immigration. Thus, model A' would not apply to an investigation that spans more than 1 year. In model B, survival is time-specific and capture probability is not, it is constant. In model D both survival and capture probability are constant with time. There is no model C, corresponding to constant survival, recapture probability varying with time. The fifth model is referred to as model 2. (No, there is no model 1.) This model is appropriate if there is trap-shyness (i.e., net avoidance) following first capture. In this case, the program does not use information from individuals between their first capture and the subsequent capture period. It is assumed that by the time of the second capture period following first capture, trap-shyness has disappeared. The disadvantage of model 2 is that a sizable portion of the data are excluded from calculations of survival and capture probability.

JOLLYAGE incorporates three of the above models, adapted to two age classes: these are referred to as A2, B2 and D2. In all these models, survival, but not capture probability is allowed to vary between the age classes. JOLLY and JOLLYAGE allow goodness-of-fit tests for a particular model. All the programs discussed above calculate confidence intervals. However, JOLLY and JOLLYAGE allow the upper confidence limit for capture or survival probability to exceed 1.0 (which is impossible) and allow the lower limit to be less than 0.0 (which is also impossible).

Design

Placement of nets and mist-net stations is described by Ralph et al. (1993) and DeSante et al. (1993). Different design considerations apply to the study of productivity as compared to the study of adult survival. In the case of productivity, the unit of analysis is the mist-net station, often containing 10 mist-nets. With pilot data in hand, one can determine the minimum number of mist-net stations needed to achieve acceptable statistical power or precision. Analyses can be conducted, either on individual species (DeSante et al. 1993, Nur et al. 1994, Johnson and Geupel 1996, Chase et al. 1997) or on groups of species (DeSante and Geupel 1987); examples of both methods were described in Example 4. Power will strongly depend on the number of individuals caught per station. Clearly, pooling species (e.g., on the basis of habitat preference), will improve statistical power. For analyses of productivity, power, and necessary sample size to achieve a stated level of power, can be calculated with standard methods (see above). For analysis of linear trends in space or time, the reader can use specialized programs, such as TRENDS and MONITOR, described above, or use a more general program, such as PASS.

For analyses of adult survival, the unit of analysis is the individual bird (adult). More precisely, the unit of analysis is the individual capture/recapture history. Since recapture is a binary event—an individual is either recaptured or it is not—power and necessary sample size can be estimated, adapting methods and results from such binary processes. Fleiss (1981) provides an easy to use text. To estimate necessary sample size (here, number of different individuals initially caught), it is necessary to know the average recapture rate (among all individuals caught in a given year, the proportion of individuals recaught in a subsequent year).

Table 12. Summary of models in JOLLY and JOLLYAGE (Pollack et al. 1990).

Program	Model	Parameters	Description
JOLLY	A	phi_i, p_i	Full Jolly-Seber model
	A'	phi_i, p_i	Jolly-Seber "death only" model
	B	phi_i, p	Time-specific survival and constant capture probablity
	D	phi, p	Constant survival and capture probability
	2	phi_i, phi^*_i, p_i	Jolly-Seber model with "trap-response"
JOLLY AGE	A2	phi_i, phi_i', p_i	2-age, time-specific survival and capture probability
	B2	phi, phi', p_i	2-age, constant survival, time-specific capture probability
	D2	phi, phi', p	2-age, constant survival and capture probability

Preliminary results from the Palomarin Field station (Nur & Geupel 1993a, Chase et al. 1997, Geupel and Nur unpublished data) and elsewhere (DeSante et al. 1993), indicate that, under favorable conditions, 30% of adults caught in one year can be expected to be recaught in the next year. We assume that transient individuals (see below) are eliminated from the analysis. The recapture rate may easily be greater or less than that, but is likely to vary between 20 and 45%.

Fleiss (1981) gives an extensive table for determining sample size necessary to detect significant effects, as a function of the recapture rate (here assumed to be proportional to survival) of two groups—e.g., two different treatments or two habitats. For example, if recapture rate of group 1 is 0.20 and the recapture rate of group 2 is 0.40 (i.e., group 2 is twice as likely to be recaught as group 1), the necessary sample to achieve 80% power to detect an effect at the 0.05 level is 91 for each group, or 182 in total. This would represent about 55 recaptured individuals, in all (=182 × .3). If one were willing to settle for 50% power, one could drop the sample size to 50 individuals caught for each group. Also, if one wished to detect a significant difference, with 80% power, when one group is 50% more likely to survive than another, while keeping the average recapture rate at 30% (i.e., recapture of 24% vs. 36%), this would require sample sizes of 323 individuals for each group (or 646, in total). These results and others summarized in Fleiss (1981) can provide guidance in designing a study. In some cases, the desired sample size will probably be achieved by using data over multiple years.

As noted above, capture-recapture analyses require more data than many other types of analysis. This is so for two reasons: (1) more data are required to estimate two parameters (survival and capture probability are separately estimated) than just one parameter, and (2) capture-recapture analyses rely on maximum-likelihood methods, unlike ANOVA and linear regression, which do not (Kleinbaum et al. 1988). The maximum-likelihood method can only work as intended when the estimate in question is greater than 0 and less than 1, assuming we are considering probability estimates, whose minimum and maximum are 0 and 1. That is, the method breaks down when an estimate falls on a boundary (in this case 0 or 1). Examples where this boundary problem comes up are: (i) you band 20 individuals of species x and none are ever recaptured, or (ii) all 20 individuals of species x are recaptured. It may seem unlikely that during the course of a multi-year study one obtains 0% recaptures or 100% recaptures, but such outcomes are not unlikely on a year-by-year basis. Thus, sampling error alone can lead to a situation where all individuals captured in a particular year are either re-sighted or no individuals are re-sighted. This presents a problem if one wishes to examine year-by-year variation in survival.

Problems can also arise in estimating capture probability. Suppose 20 individuals are captured and released in year 1. In year 2, five of these individuals are recaught, and in year 3, two of the five are recaught a second time. However, 15 of those caught and released in year 1 are never seen in year 2 or year 3. We don't know how many of those 15 actually died by year 2 and how many were alive but were missed that year. If there were one or more individuals caught in year 1, missed in year 2, and then caught again in year 3 (or later), we would have enough information to try and estimate capture probability. But in the example given, the capture-recapture analysis is forced to estimate that the capture probability is 100%. That estimate is problematic, first because it presents difficulty for the maximum likelihood method, and second, because such an estimate is likely to be biologically incorrect. We therefore recommend that capture-recapture analyses be conducted on data sets that have at least one (but preferably more than one) individual with gaps in their recapture histories (e.g. "101" or "1001"). Here "dataset" would refer to captures from a single species at a single site. The reader is referred to Cooch et al. (1996) for further discussion.

IV. Demographic Monitoring: Nest-monitoring

Nest-monitoring provides detailed information on a number of different aspects of reproductive success, in addition to potentially providing information on density, habitat associations, and other ecological characteristics (Table 1). The following components of reproductive success of a particular species may be studied: clutch initiation dates (or other aspects of breeding season chronology), number of nest attempts and/or broods reared per pair, clutch size, brood size, hatchability (proportion of eggs that hatch), number of young fledged, number of young fledged per pair, proportion of nests that fail, and nest survivorship (Martin 1992, Martin and Geupel 1993, Ralph et al. 1993). In this section we limit attention to nest survivorship. With regard to the other elements of reproductive success, their analysis is relatively straight forward and does not present any unusual difficulties. Some of these components of reproductive success can be analyzed using standard linear model analysis. The assumptions of such analysis must be met, for example, the assumption that residuals are normally distributed. Where the outcome is binary, e.g., a brood is scored "0" if it fails to produce young, and "1" if it produces one or more young, logistic regression (Chapter V) can be used. The reader is referred to several recent papers which have analyzed reproductive success (Geupel & DeSante 1990, Martin 1992, Sherry & Holmes 1993, Nur & Geupel 1993b, Robinson et al. 1995).

Background

In nest-monitoring studies, analysis of nest survivorship is usually carried out by the Mayfield method (Mayfield 1961, Mayfield 1975). Important contributions to these analysis were made by Johnson (1979) and Hensler & Nichols (1981). Recently, Pollock & Cornelius (1988) and Bromaghin & McDonald (1993) have developed alternative methods. We discuss two methods that provide good alternatives to the Mayfield method, though neither has yet been widely adopted. The first is the method of Bromaghin & McDonald (1993), which they call "Systematic Nest-searching," and the second is often termed "time-to-failure" analysis. However, the Mayfield (1961, 1975) method is at present the most widely used.

Analysis

If all nests are discovered upon initiation (e.g., before egg-laying has begun) and then followed until they succeed or fail, then it is not necessary to use the Mayfield method to estimate nest survivorship. In that case, one can score each nest as successful or not, and data can be analyzed with logistic regression, discriminant analysis or other methods. However, for many field studies, nests are usually found at various stages of the nesting cycle, and, furthermore, the ultimate fate of each nest is not always known. With such incomplete information, it is recommended to use the Mayfield (1961, 1975) method to estimate nest survivorship (but see below for analytic methods that assume that nests can be aged upon discovery). The Mayfield method consists of dividing the number of nests known to have failed by the sum of the number of days during which nests were observed and at risk of failing (equals "exposure-days"). This provides an estimate of daily nest mortality and is used to estimate nest survivorship for a particular stage of the nesting period (if one wishes to estimate stage-specific survival probability) or for the entire nesting period.

We consider it useful to summarize the following guidelines to facilitate nest survivorship analysis based on Mayfield (1961, 1975). To be included in calculations of nest success a nest must be observed a minimum of 2 times and the outcome (its fate) must be known, or at least must be established for the last observation of that nest.

Typically the nesting period is divided in to three stages: egg laying, incubation, and nestling periods. Occasionally nest building is differentiated as a fourth stage; however, in the absence of observed eggs it is difficult to distinguish early predation from failure to lay eggs. Therefore, nest survivorship is normally only determined from the point that the first egg is laid (or as soon as possible thereafter). For most passerines, one egg is laid per day, and incubation assumed to begin when the last egg is laid, with the nestling period beginning when the first egg hatches. In general, when there is no other information, the mid-point between nest checks is used as an estimate of the timing of significant events occurring in the nesting cycle. It is important to check nests regularly (once every

3-4 days is recommended) to accurately determine whether a nest survived a particular stage, or at what stage it failed (Martin & Geupel 1993).

Because nest success varies from stage to stage of the nesting cycle (Mayfield 1975) success is typically calculated as a daily rate for each one of the three periods. This daily rate is then raised exponentially according to the number of days known to occur for each period (Example 8) and for the total nest period which provides an estimate of overall survivorship probability.

When a nest found during incubation fails before hatching, the following formula can be used to estimate the first date of incubation (Martin et al. 1997):

$$\text{First day of incubation} = \text{date found} - \left(\left(\text{incubation period} - \text{number of days observed} \right) \div 2 \right)$$

Species-specific lengths of the incubation and nestling period may be obtained from the published literature (Baicich and Harrison 1997). After a few years of field study, site-specific information on periods should be substituted as it may vary among sites.

To establish confidence limits and compare variances and statistical significance of differences in survivorship values we follow recommendations made by Johnson (1979), illustrated with an example from his paper.

Example 8:
Variances and Confidence Interval of Nest Survivorship
During incubation, 154 nests of Kirtland's Warblers (*Dendroica kirtlandii*) were discovered and of these 35 were observed to fail and 119 successfully completed incubation. These 154 nests were active and observed for a total of 882.5 days. A nest that is found on 1 May and is still active on 10 May is credited with 9 days of exposure. A nest that is found on 1 May and is found to have been destroyed on 10 May is credited with 4.5 days of exposure on the assumption that predation occurred in the mid-point of the period, and therefore that it survived 4.5 days of exposure. The estimate of daily mortality probability is n/E, where n = number of nests failing and E = total number of exposure days for successful and unsuccessful nests.

Here n/E = 35/882.5 = 0.040. Thus, the daily survival probability for the incubation period = s = 1 – 0.04 = 0.96. Over a 14 day period (the length of incubation) this is equivalent to 0.96^{14} or a survivorship of 0.565.

The standard error of the daily survival probability (= standard error of the daily mortality probability) is the square root of the variance of s. The formula for the variance of s is:

$$\text{Var(s)} = \frac{(E-n)(n)}{E^3}$$

where E and n are as defined above. In this example, the standard error of s = 0.00657. One can construct a confidence interval using the mean and standard error and assuming approximation to a normal distribution (Sokal and Rohlf 1995, Zar 1996) and then exponentiate to obtain a confidence interval for the entire incubation period (in this species, 14 days long). The 95% confidence interval for daily nest survival is 0.96–1.96*0.00657 for the lower bound and 0.96+1.96*0.00657 for the upper bound; thus, the 95% confidence interval for nest-survivorship during the incubation period is (0.467, 0.684). Note that while the confidence interval around the daily nest survival rate is symmetric (about 0.96), the confidence interval around total nest survivorship is not symmetric: the upper bound is 0.119 above 0.565, while the lower bound is 0.098 below 0.565.

As recommended by Johnson (1979), one can compare two independent samples with regard to nest-survivorship to determine if the two are significantly different by using a Z-test. That is, one can construct a Z score (analogous to a t-statistic when using a t test) and compare this to a "normal" deviate, one with mean = 0 and variance = 1. One can then evaluate whether the Z score obtained is significantly different from zero as follows. The difference in estimates of daily nest survival (= difference in daily nest mortality) can be evaluated with the following formula:

$$Z = \frac{s_1 - s_2}{\sqrt{\text{Var}(s_1) + \text{Var}(s_2)}}$$

where s_1 and s_2 refer to daily nest survival in group 1 and group 2, respectively. The P-values associated with respective Z scores are easily obtained from standard texts or from statistical software; e.g., Z = +1.96 corresponds to a two-tailed P-value of 0.05, as does Z = –1.96.

For analysis of nest survival rate, the biologist can use the program CONTRAST (Sauer and Williams 1989). This program allows for multiple comparisons, not just comparisons of two groups as described above.

Additional Considerations

Careful attention to field protocol can keep observer-induced predation to a minimum (Martin and Geupel 1993, review in Göttmark 1992). One method to examine the influence of an observer's finding nests on nest-predation (Martin and Geupel 1993), is to vary the number of days (between 1 and 4) elapsing between nest-discovery and the first subsequent check; one then compares the proportion failing after 1, 2, 3 or 4 days since the first visit. In the absence of observer impact, the proportion failing should be $1-s$, $1-s^2$, $1-s^3$ and $1-s^4$, where s is the daily probability of nest survival (the parameter estimated by the Mayfield method). Thus if $s = 0.97$, we expect 3% should fail after 1 day, 5.9% would fail during a 2 day period, 8.7% fail during a 3 day period, and 11.5% fail during a 4 day period. This comparison can be made during the breeding season, as a check on a particular observer or a particular species, to see if it is unusually sensitive to disturbance. In this case, s may not be known, but there should be, in the absence of an observer-effect, about four times the number of failed nests after 4 days (since nest-locating) as after 1 day. If this proportionality is violated, an observer-impact is to be suspected. Studies examining observer impact directly have generally found little evidence of increased nest failure among passerines due to observer disturbance (Göttmark 1992, Ortega et al. 1997).

Pooling data across species is not recommended. This is especially important if (a) species differ with respect to length of nest period, or (b) species differ with respect to daily survival probability. The Mayfield method assumes the absence of such heterogeneity, and its existence would violate this assumption. Even if species do not differ with respect to (a) or (b) they may still differ with respect to other relevant life-history traits or ecological characteristics, hence it would be preferable to make separate calculations for each species and use these species-specific estimates in subsequent statistical analyses. For example, one might compare the importance of nest-location (ground vs. shrub nesters), by comparing survival estimates for each of five species that nest on the ground with five species that nest in shrubs (assuming the two groups of species do not differ with respect to another, confounding factor), even though sample size of each species may be small.

Alternatives to the Mayfield Method: Systematic Searching and Time-to-Failure Analysis

One of the advantages of the Mayfield method is its flexibility. Thus, the Mayfield method could be used in the absence of systematic nest-searching and nest-monitoring. For example, an investigator could analyze data in which the interval between

successive nest visits varied widely (perhaps due to availability of personnel). At the same time this very asset of the Mayfield method can become a drawback, if nest-monitoring is actually being conducted in a systematic fashion. In the latter case, the Mayfield method will not be an efficient estimator; i.e., estimates of nest survivorship will be less precise than can be achieved using other methods. In this section we briefly mention two alternative approaches to estimating nest survivorship using the Mayfield Method. The first, "Systematic searching," was developed by Bromaghin & McDonald (1993). Their approach assumes that all potential nest sites in the sampled area are searched at regular intervals (e.g., every 4 days). They also assume: (1) nests can be aged when discovered (at least approximately), and (2) all nests, once discovered, are monitored until they succeed (e.g., fledge at least one young) or fail. These assumptions are more restrictive than the Mayfield method, but they allow one to estimate nest survivorship more precisely than possible with the Mayfield method. Aging nests is not necessarily difficult; even nests found during the incubation stage can be aged, as discussed by Lokemoen and Koford (1996). Readers may request the program ENCOUNTR from Bromaghin and McDonald, which will implement the analytic methods (address for Jeffrey Bromaghin: Alaska Dept. of Fish & Game, 333 Raspberry Road, Anchorage, AK 99518).

The second alternative is referred to as "time-to-failure" analysis, also "survival analysis." This body of analysis is derived from the Cox Proportional Hazards Model (Cox & Oakes 1984, Kalbfleisch & Prentice 1980) though it is not restricted to that particular model. It has the advantage of allowing sophisticated statistical modeling, and makes fewer assumptions than the Mayfield method (e.g., it does not assume time-constant survival rates). It allows nests to be included in the analysis for which ultimate fate is unknown (these are referred to as "censored" observations). It does assume, like the method of Bromaghin & McDonald (1993), that nests can be aged upon discovery. We know of no published applications of survival analysis to nest survivorship. Many general statistical packages have the capability to implement this type of analysis, including STATA and EGRET (addresses for which have been given above), S-PLUS (address: MathSoft, 1700 Westlake Ave. N, Suite 500, Seattle, WA 98109) and SAS.

Vegetation Analysis in Relation to Nest-monitoring

An example of combining analysis of vegetation features in relation to nest success and choice of nest substrate is provided by Martin & Roper (1988), who investigated nest and vegetation features of Hermit Thrushes (*Catharus guttatus*) breeding in central

Arizona. Habitat data were collected, using a modification of the James & Shugart (1980) protocol, within a 5-m radius circle centered on each nest (use-site) and at non-use sites centered on a point 50 m distant from a Hermit Thrush nest, but within the same micro-habitat type. Habitat variables included the number of small white firs (between 1 and 3 m tall), number of all small conifers, number of all large conifers, number of maple stems categorized by size, number of locust stems categorized by size, and total number of deciduous woody stems. Nests were also classified according to whether they did ("low" predation) or did not ("high" predation) escape predation during the egg stage.

Martin & Roper (1988) found that Hermit Thrush use and non-use sites were distinguished only by number of small white firs: use sites averaged 17.5 small firs per plot while non-use sites, though in the same micro-habitat type, averaged 7.6 small firs per plot (P = 0.006). Once this variable was included in a stepwise discriminant analysis no other habitat variable contributed significantly to explaining differences between the two types of sites.

Stepwise discriminant analysis identified two important habitat variables that together accounted for differences in predation category: number of small white firs and minimum measure of nest cover visible from the side. Nests with low predation rates had more small firs and more cover than nests with high predation rates. Martin & Roper (1988) infer that Hermit Thrush nest-site preference for small white firs has evolved in response to predation pressure that is stronger, the fewer the number of small white firs. A similar analysis can be performed by logistic regression (Kleinbaum et al. 1988), without requiring as many assumptions as does discriminant analysis.

Design

An important consideration is the desirable sample size, usually the number of nests. Hensler & Nichols (1981) provide a table of sample size needed to estimate nest survivorship for various parameter values: length of nesting period, daily survival probability of a nest, and degree of precision desired. Precision was measured as v/s where s = daily survival probability (= 1 − daily mortality probability) and v is the standard error of s. For example with $s = 0.95$ and $v = 0.0095$, $v/s = 0.01$. In this example, an approximate 95% confidence interval for s would have a lower value of 0.931 (=0.95 − 1.96*0.0095) and an upper value of 0.969 (=0.95 + 1.96*0.0095). Translated into survival probabilities for the entire nesting period (of J days), would yield an average (mean) survival probability of 0.95^J, with a lower confidence bound of 0.931^J and an upper confidence bound of 0.969^J. If J

= 25, then the mean is 0.28 and the lower and upper bounds are (0.17,0.45). If J = 30 and daily survival probability is 0.98, the mean is 0.545 and the lower and upper bounds are (0.30,0.98). Thus, it can be seen that a precision of 0.01 is very crude indeed; it allows one to specify only a very broad interval for survival probability during the nesting period, e.g., 30% to 98%.

Hensler & Nichols (1981) calculate that to achieve a precision of 0.01 (as defined above), with daily survival probability = 0.97 and nesting period (J) = 30, would require a sample of 23 nests. The confidence interval for s^J is very broad: between 22% and 72%, with the mean = 40%. If the desired precision is 0.005, the lower and upper bounds are tighter, lying between 29 and 53%. Such precision would require 93 nests. If J is lower, necessary sample size increases; if J is greater, necessary sample sizes would decrease. Also, with higher daily survival probability, sample size decreases and conversely, with lower daily survival probability, necessary sample sizes increase. It is possible to obtain precision of 0.005 with a sample of 27 nests (assuming a nesting period of 30 days), but this would require a daily survival probability of 0.99, which implies nest survival over the whole (30 day) period is 0.74, a value that is unattainable for most open-cup nesters, but may be reasonable for cavity nesters (Martin and Li 1992).

Hensler & Nichols (1981) also provide some power calculations in relation to sample size, nestling period and daily survival probability. They assumed two groups of equal sample size were being compared; daily nest survival for group 1 = s_1; daily nest survival for group 2 = s_2. Their power calculations for $\alpha = 0.05$ are shown in Table 13, for s_1 = 0.95; J = 20, 30 or 40; and K = number of nests in each group = 20, 75 and 500. s_2 varied from 0.04 less than s_1 to as much as 0.04 greater than s_2 (provided that s_2 was less than 1.0). The results in Table 13 indicate, first of all, that 20 nests per groups is almost never sufficient to achieve reasonable power (here defined as 60% power), except when the effect (difference between daily nest survivorship) was very large. For example, with K = 20 nests, s_1 = 0.95, and J = 20 days, the 60% power criterion is never attained. Changing J to 30, instead, resulted in 60% power or more only if s_2 was equal to 0.99. In this situation nest survivorship for the entire period was 0.21 for group 1 and equal to 0.74 for group 2, i.e., group 2 was more than three times as likely to survive as those in group 1. Finally, with J = 40 days, K = 20 nests, 73% power was attained if one group had 0.99 survival per day and the other group had 0.96 survival (equivalent to overall survivorship of 0.67 and 0.20, respectively). With K = 75 nests per group, power was 60% or more with moderate

Table 13. Power analysis for detecting differences in survivorship between two groups. Power = proportion of the times null hypothesis was rejected at the $\alpha = 0.05$ significance level (from Hensler & Nichols 1981).

J	s_1	K	\u0394 −0.040	−0.030	−0.020	−0.010	−0.005	0.0	0.005	0.010	0.020	0.030	0.040
20	0.95	20	0.26	0.24	0.13	0.06	0.07	0.02	0.05	0.06	0.21	0.30	0.67
		75	0.82	0.58	0.38	0.10	0.10	0.03	0.04	0.10	0.48	0.92	0.99
		500	1.00	1.00	0.99	0.50	0.19	0.04	0.28	0.68	0.99	1.00	1.00
30	0.95	20	0.33	0.23	0.15	0.05	0.03	0.06	0.07	0.12	0.21	0.47	0.80
		75	0.88	0.70	0.39	0.17	0.04	0.07	0.09	0.18	0.65	0.98	1.00
		500	1.00	1.00	0.99	0.69	0.20	0.08	0.23	0.83	1.00	1.00	1.00
40	0.99	20	0.90	0.73	0.49	0.24	0.07	0.03	0.03	–	–	–	–
		75	1.00	1.00	0.97	0.55	0.20	0.05	0.29	–	–	–	–
		500	1.0	1.00	1.00	1.00	0.87	0.08	1.00	–	–	–	–

100 simulations were conducted for each combination of J, s_1, K and Δ values. In each simulation, 2 groups of nests characterized by s_1 and s_2 (where $s_2 = s_1 + \Delta$) were sampled. The proportion of these simulations in which the null hypothesis ($s_1 = s_2$) is rejected is presented (for $\Delta = 0$ this estimates the significance level of the test). J denotes the nesting period and K is the number of nests observed for both of the simulated groups. For $s_1 = 0.99$, values of $\Delta \geq 0.01$ are not biologically feasible and are, thus, not presented.

differences in nest survivorship. For example, 65% power was attained provided that $s_1 = 0.95$ and $s_2 = 0.97$ (assuming J = 30); this translates to 0.21 vs. 0.40 survivorship over the whole period. Similarly, 70% power was attained with $s_1 = 0.95$ and $s_2 = 0.92$, equivalent to 0.21 and 0.08 survival, respectively over the whole period. However, even with daily mortality twice as high in one groups as the other ($s_1 = 0.99$ vs. $s_2 = 0.98$), assuming J = 40 days, and K = 75 nests per group, power was only 0.55. With K = 500 nests per group—hardly feasible for passerine studies—even small differences in nest survivorship yielded high power. For example, power was 83% comparing $s_1 = 0.95$ and $s_2 = 0.96$ (assuming J = 30 days)

Our conclusion is that 20 nests will rarely be sufficient for statistical comparisons and that 500 nests will be more than enough. 75 nests per group appears sufficient to achieve reasonable power, unless differences in nest survivorship are

subtle (difference in daily nest survival of 0.01 or less). Whereas, Hensler & Nichols (1981) provide a table to determine sample size required to achieve a specified level of precision, they do not determine sample size required to achieve a specified level of power. Inspection of Table 13, however, indicates two important points: (1) It is not possible to draw conclusions about necessary sample size to achieve specified power without considering the nesting period (J) and the baseline daily nest-survival. Therefore no simple rule of thumb can be provided. (2) Twenty nests represents a minimum sample size under the best circumstances (see comment above), but generally that number of nests (per group) will provide inadequate statistical power. Our conclusion agrees with that of Hensler and Nichols (1981) who considered the sample sizes necessary to achieve a specified level of precision: they stated that under no circumstances could they recommend a sample size of less than 20 nests.

V. Logistic Regression

Like linear regression and ANOVA, logistic regression is a broadly applicable method, one that is particularly suited for the analysis of binary outcomes; i.e., any situation in which the outcome can be can be scored either "1" or "0" and the probability of that outcome can be related to one or more independent variables. We have already briefly mentioned it in regard to analysis of presence/absence data obtained from point counts. Another example might be the analysis of environmental factors that relate to nest site selection, comparing sites with nests (scored 1) and sites without nests (scored 0). Survival of a nest to fledging is yet another example where logistic regression might be applied. Important features of logistic regression include the following:

1. Like linear regression, the outcome variable in logistic regression is modeled as a linear combination of predictor or independent variables. However, an important distinction is that because the response variable is measured on a discrete, binary level, the error term has a *binomial* distribution, not a normal distribution, as is found with linear regression. Linear regression estimates the mean of a dependent variable for a set of predictor values, while logistic regression estimates the proportion of responses in one of two possible outcomes given a set of predictor values.

2. Unlike linear regression, the outcome (e.g., survived or died, scored 1 or 0, respectively) is first transformed before being analyzed. If p refers to the probability of survival, then logistic regression analyzes the natural logarithm of $[p/(1-p)]$. Therefore $p/(1-p)$ can be thought of as the odds of survival. For example, when the probability of surviving is 0.75, the odds of surviving = 0.75/0.25 or 3, meaning that the odds of surviving are three times as great as the odds of dying. $\ln[p/(1-p)]$ is referred to as logit p. In the case of simple logistic regression (analogous to simple linear regression), the relationship being modeled is:

$$\text{logit } p = a + bx,$$

where x is the independent variable, a is the intercept for the equation and b is the regression coefficient. This relationship can be rewritten as:

$$p = \frac{e^{a+bx}}{1+e^{a+bx}}$$

It is easy to see that the relationship between p and x will be non-linear, even though the relationship between logit p and x is linear. One can use the logistic equation to provide the expected or predicted proportion of "successes" for a given x value.

3. Logistic regression makes no assumptions about the independent variables, unlike discriminant analysis (Kleinbaum et al. 1988, Ludwig & Reynolds 1988), which assumes that the independent variables are distributed as a multi-variate normal.

4. Logistic regression does, however, assume independence of outcome among all observations. Suppose we are following survival to fledgling among 100 nestlings that came from 20 broods. Each nestling is classified as having survived (scored 1) or died (scored 0). Logistic regression on the fate of the 100 nestlings would require that each nestling survive or die independently of all others, including its siblings. However, survival among siblings, especially while still in the nest, cannot be assumed to be independent but this assumption could be tested. Linear regression based on 100 observations may also be inappropriate. However, here we can collapse the data and analyze survival from 20 broods; the outcome is a number between 0 and 5. Analysis of an outcome that takes on 6 different values is not possible for standard logistic regression, in which the outcome must be 0 or 1. There are variants of logistic regression which can accommodate non-independence of observations, e.g., available in EGRET, a user-friendly, menu-driven program with an excellent, easy-to-understand manual (available from S.E.R.C., 909 Northeast 43rd St., Seattle, WA, 98105). Another variant on logistic regression is *ordered logistic regression*, which can be implemented in STATA (see address above).

Example 9:
Analysis of Presence/Absence Data Using Logistic Regression

We provide the following example of logistic regression, from a study of factors influencing abundance and distribution of Grasshopper Sparrows (*Ammodramus savannarum*) and other species on a shrub- steppe and grassland site in eastern Oregon (Holmes & Geupel 1998). Holmes and Geupel (1998) analyzed the presence or absence of Grasshopper Sparrows at 220 point count stations over a 3 year period in relation to a suite of habitat and vegetation features. Here we focus on data from the 141 point counts situated in shrub, in relation to the influence of three habitat variables: perennial grass cover, overall shrub cover, and density of big sagebrush (*Artemesia tridentata*). Considered one at a time, each is strongly associated with the presence (in the case of perennial grass) or absence (in the case of shrub cover and *Artemesia tridentata*) of Grasshopper Sparrows. Annotated statistical results output from STATA from the single-variable logistic regression analyses are presented in Table 14 (A, B, and C).

1. The likelihood ratio statistic (LRS), degrees of freedom (in parentheses), and associated P-value are presented for the overall model. Under the null hypothesis, the LRS is distributed as a chi-squared statistic, hence STATA labels the statistic "chi2(df)." However, because the LRS is a different statistic from the "usual" chi squared statistic (Pearson goodness-of-fit), we prefer to label it LRS.

2. STATA presents a statistic "Pseudo R^2" which is comparable to R^2 from ANOVA conducted on individual observations. The interpretation of Pseudo R^2 is the same as the usual R^2: it is the proportion of variation in the dependent variable accounted for by the independent variable or variables. In this case, 31% of variation in presence or absence of Grasshopper Sparrows at individual point count stations can be accounted for by an index of perennial grass cover.

3. The log likelihood of the model is presented. We refer the reader to texts such as Kleinbaum et al. (1988) for more extensive discussion of log likelihood. For every statistical model a likelihood can be calculated which measures how well that model accounts for the observed outcomes. Because the likelihood is a number less than 1, the log likelihood is always negative. Thus, the more negative the log likelihood, the more *poorly* does that model account for the observed variation in the dependent variable. Comparing Table 14A and 14C we see that the model with perennial grass cover accounts for more of the variation in Grasshopper Sparrow presence and absence than

does the model with *Artemesia* only: the former has a less negative log likelihood and, consequently, a greater Psuedo R^2.

4. The logistic regression coefficient and its standard error are shown. The results imply that an increase in the log(perennial grass cover) index of one unit increases the logit(p) by +2.28 units, where p refers to the presence of Grasshopper Sparrows at that point count station.

5. STATA provides a statistical test for the significance of each independent variable in the model. This test is referred to as a Wald test. However, this test is *not* recommended (Hosmer and Lemeshow 1989), because the nominal P-value does not correspond well to actual P-value. In some cases, the P-value from the Wald test is too high, leading to a Type II error. Instead, the Likelihood Ratio Test and its associated statistic, LRS, is recommended for statistical inference (Kleinbaum et al. 1988, Lebreton et al. 1992). Essentially, the Wald test provides a quick and easy test of the P-value for an independent variable. The problem is that using this quick and easy estimate is often unreliable.

The relationship between Grasshopper Sparrow presence and perennial grass cover is shown graphically in Figure 5, showing the predicted probability of Grasshopper Sparrow presence (over the course of the 3 year study), derived from the statistical model in Table 14A. This shows (Figure 5) the actual percentages of occurrence of Grasshopper Sparrows in relation to the perennial grass cover index (PGCI) at each point count station. These percentages of Grasshopper Sparrow occurrence were obtained by grouping point count stations that had similar PGCI values. An index value of 0 (which corresponds to 0% perennial grass cover) and the probability of detecting one or more Grasshopper Sparrows at that point count station over a 3 year period was about 30%. The probability of detecting a Grasshopper Sparrow increased to 40 to 50% with a small increase in the PGCI to a value of 0.5. With a PGCI value of 1 (corresponding to a perennial grass cover of 1%), the probability of detecting a Grasshopper Sparrow increases to over 70%. With a PGCI value of 1.5 (corresponding to a perennial grass cover of 3%), the probability of detecting a Grasshopper exceeds 90%. And by the time the PGCI reaches 2.0 (corresponding to a perennial grass cover of over 5%), the probability of detecting a Grasshopper Sparrow at that point count station approaches 100%.

Having obtained the results in Table 14 A, B, and C, the investigator may wish to conduct a multiple logistic regression analysis to determine how many different factors may be contributing to variation in

Table 14. Logistic regression analysis of Grasshopper Sparrow presence/absence in relation to habitat features (from Holmes & Geupel 1998). Dependent variable is detection of Grasshopper Sparrow at any of 9 surveys (scored as "1"), conducted at 141 point count stations. A. Simple logistic regression in relation to Perennial Grass. B. Simple logistic regression in relation to shrub cover. C. Simple logistic regression in relation to *Artemesia* Density. D. Multiple logistic regression analysis with all 3 independent variables. E. Best, multiple logistic regression model, and associated goodness-of-fit statistics.

A) Independent Variable: Perennial Grass Cover Index [lpergras] = ln(Perennial Grass Cover + 1),
where Perennial Grass Cover is measured on 0 to 100 scale

Logit Estimates
③

Log Likelihood = –67.584999

	Coef.	Std. Err.	z	P>|z|	[95% Conf. Interval]	
lpergras	2.280344	.486312	4.689	0.000	1.32719	3.233499

Number of obs = 141
① { chi2(1) = 60.23
{ Prob >chi2 = 0.0000
② Pseudo R2 = 0.3083
④ ⑤

B) Independent Variable: Shrub Cover [shrubcov] (on 0 to 100 scale)

Logit Estimates

Log Likelihood = –86.689465

Number of obs = 141
chi2(1) = 22.02
Prob >chi2 = 0.0000
Pseudo R2 = 0.1127

	Coef.	Std. Err.	z	P>|z|	[95% Conf. Interval]	
shrubcov	–.0778626	.0182709	–4.262	0.000	–.113673	–.0420522

C) Independent Variable: Density of *Artemesia* [artemden] = number of individuals

Logit Estimates

Log Likelihood = –90.154756

Number of obs = 141
chi2(1) = 15.09
Prob >chi2 = 0.0001
Pseudo R2 = 0.0772

	Coef.	Std. Err.	z	P>|z|	[95% Conf. Interval]	
artemden	–.0200667	.0055873	–3.591	0.000	–.0310177	–.0091157

D) Multiple logistic regression analysis with all 3 independent variables

Logit Estimates

Log Likelihood = –60.570704

Number of obs = 141
chi2(3) = 74.26
Prob >chi2 = 0.0000
Pseudo R2 = 0.3800

	Coef.	Std. Err.	z	P>|z|	[95% Conf. Interval]	
lpergras	2.797955	.7079792	3.952	0.000	1.410342	4.185569
shrubcov	–.0215319	.0252564	–0.853	0.394	–.0710336	.0279697
artemden	–.0198948	.0081006	–2.456	0.014	–.0357716	–.004018
_cons	–.1434713	.496225	–0.289	0.772	–1.116054	.8291118

Likelihood Ratio Test for each independent variable while controlling for the other two:
lpergras LRS = 50.37, df=1, P <0.0001
shrubcov LRS = 0.74, df=1, P = 0.39
artemden LRS = 6.50, df=1, P =0.011

E) Best multiple logistic regression model

Logit Estimates

Log Likelihood = –60.938791

Number of obs = 141
chi2(2) = 73.53
Prob >chi2 = 0.0000
Pseudo R2 = 0.3763

	Coef.	Std. Err.	z	P>|z|	[95% Conf. Interval]	
lpergras	2.846168	.7031315	4.048	0.000	1.468056	4.224281
artemden	–.0231516	.0070722	–3.274	0.001	–.0370129	–.0092903
_cons	–.4889746	.2930915	–1.668	0.095	–1.063423	.0854741

Likelihood Ratio Test for each independent variable while controlling for the other:
lpergras LRS = 58.43, df=1, P <0.0001
artemden LRS = 13.29, df=1, P <0.001

Hosmer-Lemeshow Goodness of Fit test for above model:
number of observations   =   141
number of groups   =   15
Hosmer-Lemeshow chi2(13)   =   6.21
Prob >chi2   =   0.938

the presence of Grasshopper Sparrows. The approach is parallel to that used in ordinary multiple regression analysis (Example 4). Table 14D shows results from a model in which all 3 independent variables are included. Table 14E shows both the results of the Wald test for the three independent variables and below that the results of the Likelihood Ratio Test for each of the three independent variables. Here we see that, with *artemden* and *lpergras* in the model, shrubcov does not contribute significantly to explaining variation in the presence of Grasshopper Sparrows. In this case results were similar whether we relied on the Wald test or the Likelihood Ratio Test. We therefore run another model, with only *lpergras* and *artemden* included, shown in Table 14E. In this case, we see that the effect of each of the 2 variables is significant when controlling for the effect of the other. Note that the Pseudo R^2 for the 2-variable model is 0.376 compared to the Pseudo R^2 of 0.308 for *lpergras* alone. Thus, by including *artemden* in the model we were able to increase the Pseudo R^2 by about 7%.

If we select a multiple logistic regression model (Table 14E), we should also examine the goodness of fit of that model. STATA conducts a goodness of fit test based on Hosmer and Lemeshow (1989). We find no reason to reject the fit of the model ($P>0.9$ in this case), implying that the assumption made in logistic regression that residuals are binomially distributed is satisfied. If we had obtained a significant lack of fit (i.e., $P <0.05$) this would cause us to question the validity of the model. Lack of fit may arise from non-independence of observations, or failure to include in the logistic regression model an important variable which explains variation in the outcome variable.

Statistical texts that include a discussion of logistic regression include Cox & Snell (1989) and Hosmer & Lemeshow (1989). There is no text oriented towards field biology that discusses logistic regression, but the reader is referred to Sydeman et al. (1991), Trexler & Travis (1993), Crawley (1993) and Spear & Nur (1994) for discussion and applications using field data. Logistic regression is widely available in major statistical packages. A clearly explained and flexible implementation of logistic regression is available in the program EGRET (address provided above).

Figure 5. Probability of detecting Grasshopper Sparrows in relation to Index of Perennial Grass Cover.

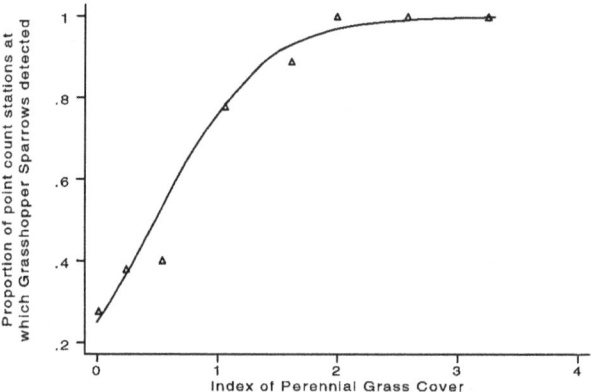

Figure 5. Probability of detecting Grasshopper Sparrows at 141 individual point count stations in relation to Index of Perennial Grass Cover (from Holmes & Geupel 1998) (statistical analysis in Table 14). The index = ln(percent cover that is perennial grass + 1). Point count stations have been grouped and the proportion of stations at which one or more Grasshopper Sparrows were detected is shown (triangles); also shown is the logistic regression line of best fit.

VI. Concluding Remarks

We conceived of this Statistical Guide as a jumping-off point for biologists wishing to design and analyze data from population monitoring programs. We recognize that we have presented less detail on some points or areas than some readers would like, and therefore have recommended texts, or other references, that consider more specialized topics in greater detail. Our objective has been to provide guideposts, not to provide an encyclopedic treatment of statistical analysis and design. Statistical analysis is a field that progresses rapidly, and thus analytic methods that were recommended a decade or two ago have now been superseded. We expect that methods that are only now being considered (e.g., application of time-to-failure analyses) will be commonplace in a few years. Other analytic methods which interested readers should consider, but which we have devoted little space to, include: bootstrapping and other re-sampling methods, Poisson regression analysis, generalized linear models, and distance-sampling.

Computer programs evolve even faster than analytic methods, and we have tried to provide current information, but recognize that such information becomes obsolete very quickly. For this reason, we recognize that a Guide such as this is most useful when it remains current. Therefore, we encourage readers to send comments and corrections to the senior author, so as to improve the quality of the next versions.

References

Anderson-Sprecher, R. 1994. Model comparisons and R^2. Am. Statistician 48:113-117.

Arnason, A.N. and C.J. Schwarz. 1986. POPAN-3: extended analysis and testing features for POPAN-2. Charles Babbage Research Centre, St. Pierre, Manitoba, Canada.

Baicich, P.J. and C.J.O. Harrison. 1997. A guide to the nests, eggs, and nestlings of North America, 2nd ed. Academic Press, San Diego, CA.

Bart, J. and W. Notz. 1996. Analysis of data. *In* T.A. Bookhout (ed.), Research and management techniques for wildlife and habitats, 5th ed. The Wildl. Soc., Bethesda, MD.

Bart, J., M. Fligner, and W. Notz. 1998. Sampling and statistical methods for behavioral ecologists. Cambridge Univ. Press, England.

Bibby, C.J., N.D. Burgess, and D.A. Hill. 1992. Bird census techniques. Academic Press, London, England.

Bromaghin, J.F. and L.L. McDonald. 1993. A systematic-encounter-sampling design for nesting studies. Auk 110:646-651.

Brownie, C., D.R. Anderson, K.P. Burnham, and D.S. Robson. 1985. Statistical inference from band recovery data-a handbook. U.S. DOI Fish & Wildl. Serv., Resource Publi. 156.

Buckland, S.T. 1980. A modified analysis of the Jolly-Seber capture-recapture model. Biometrics 36:419-435.

Buckland, S.T., D.R. Anderson, K.P. Burnham, and J.L. Laake. 1993. Distance sampling: estimating abundance of biological populations. Chapman & Hall, London, England.

Burnham, K.P., D.R. Anderson, G.C. White, C. Brownie, and K.H. Pollock. 1987. Design and analysis methods for fish survival experiments based on release-recapture. Am. Fisheries Soc. Monogr. 5.

Butcher, G.S. 1992. Needs Assessment: monitoring neotropical migratory birds. Unpubl. report for *Partners in Flight*, Ithaca, NY.

Chase, M., N. Nur, and G. R. Geupel. 1997. Survival, productivity, and abundance of a Wilson's Warbler population. Auk 114:354-366.

Cohen, J. 1988. Statistical power analysis for the behavioral sciences, 2nd ed. Lawrence Erlbaum Associates, Hillsdale, NJ.

Clobert, J., J.D. Lebreton and D. Allainé. 1987. A general approach to survival rate estimation by recaptures or resightings of marked birds. Ardea 75:133-42.

Cooch, E., R. Pradel, and N. Nur. 1996. A practical guide to mark-recapture analysis using SURGE. Centre d'Ecologie Fonctionelle et Evolutive, CNRS, Montpellier, France.

Cox, D.R. and D. Oakes. 1984. Analysis of survival data. Chapman and Hall, London, England.

Cox, D.R. and E.J. Snell. 1989. Analysis of binary data. Chapman and Hall, London, England.

Crawley, M.J. 1993. GLIM for ecologists. Blackwell Scientific, Oxford, England.

Dawson, D.G. 1981. Experimental design when counting birds. *In* C. J. Ralph and J. M. Scott (eds.), Estimating numbers of terrestrial birds. Stud. in Avian Biol. No. 6.

DeSante, D.F, K.M. Burton, and O.E. Williams. 1993. The monitoring avian productivity and survivorship (MAPS) program second annual report. Bird Populations 1:1- 28.

DeSante, D.F., and G.R. Geupel. 1987. Landbird productivity in central coastal California: the relationship to annual rainfall and a reproductive failure in 1986. Condor 89:636-653.

Dieni, J.S. 1996. The effects of burning on breeding bird community structure in aspen forests. Ms. Thesis, Univ. of Wyoming, Laramie.

Draper, N.R. and H. Smith. 1981. Applied regression analysis, 2nd ed. John Wiley, NY.

Ellison, A.M. 1992. Statistics for PCs. Bull. Ecol. Soc. of Am. 73:74-87.

Erdfelder, E., F. Faul, and A. Buchner. 1996. GPOWER: a general power analysis program. Behaviour Research Methods, Instruments, and Computers 28:1-11.

Fleiss, J. L. 1981. Statistical methods for rates and proportions, 2d ed. Wiley & Sons, NY.

Gerrodette, T. 1987. A power analysis for detecting trends. Ecology 68:1364-1372.

Gerrodette, T. 1991. Models of power of detecting trends—a reply to Link and Hatfield. Ecology 72:1889-1892.

Geupel, G.R. and D.F. DeSante, 1990. Incidence and determinants of double brooding in Wrentits. Condor 92:67-75.

Geupel, G.R. and I. Warkentin. 1995. Field methods for monitoring population parameters of landbirds in Mexico. *In* M. Wilson and S. Saeder (eds.), Conservation of neotropical migrant birds in Mexico. Maine Agricult. and For. Experiment Stat. Misc. Publi. 727, Orono, ME.

Göttmark, F. 1992. The effects of investigator disturbance on nesting birds. Current Ornithol. 9:63-104.

Greenwood, J.J.D. 1996. Basic techniques. *In* W.J. Sutherland (ed.), Ecological census techniques. Cambridge Univ. Press, England.

Gutzwiller, K.J. and H.A. Marcum. 1997. Bird reactions to observer clothing color: implications for distance-sampling techniques. J. Wildl. Manage. 61:935-947.

Hays, R.L., C. Summers, and W. Seitz. 1981. Estimating wildlife habitat variables. U.S. DOI, Fish & Wildl. Serv., FWS/OBS-8147, Washington, D.C.

Hensler, G.L. and J.D. Nichols. 1981. The Mayfield method of estimating nesting success: a model, estimators and simulation results. Wilson Bull. 93:42-53.

Hicks, C.R. 1982. Fundamental concepts in the design of experiments, 3rd ed. Holt, Rinehart and Winston, NY.

Holmes, A. and G.R. Geupel. 1998. Avian population studies at the Naval Weapons Systems Training Facility, Boardman, Oregon. Unpubl. final report of the Point Reyes Bird Observatory to U.S. Navy and Oregon Department of Fish & Game. (Available from PRBO, 4990 Shoreline Highway, Stinson Beach, CA 94970.)

Hosmer, D.W. and S. Lemeshow. 1989. Applied logistic regression. Wiley & Sons, NY.

Hurlbert, S.H. 1984. Pseudoreplication and the design of ecological field experiments. Ecol. Monogr. 54:187-211.

Hutto, R.L., S.M. Pletscet, and P. Hendricks. 1986. A fixed- radius point count method for nonbreeding and breeding season use. Auk 103:593-602.

Hutto, R.L. and C. Paige, 1995. USDA Forest Service Northern Region landbird monitoring program. Unpubl. report of USDA For. Serv. (Available from Div. of Biological Science. University of Montana, Missoula, MT 59812.)

James, F.C. and H.H. Shugart, Jr. 1970. A quantitative method of habitat description. Audubon Field Notes 24:727-736.

Johnson, D.H. In Press. Statistical considerations in monitoring birds over large areas. *In* Bonney, R., D. N. Pashley, R. Cooper and L. Niles (eds.). Strategies for Bird Conservation: The *Partners in Flight* Planning Process. Proceedings of the 1995 Cape May International *Partners in Flight* Workshop. Cornell Lab of Ornithology. <http://birds.cornell.edu/pifcapemay> (Available from D. H. Johnson, NPWRC, USGS-BRD, Jamestown, ND 58401.)

Johnson, D.H. 1979. Estimating nest success: the Mayfield method and an alternative. Auk 96:651-661.

Johnson, M.D. and G.R. Geupel. 1996. The importance of productivity to the dynamics of a Swainson's Thrush population. Condor 98:133-141.

Kalbfleisch, J.D. and R.L. Prentice. 1980. The statistical analysis of time to failure data. John Wiley, NY.

Kleinbaum, D.G., L.L. Kupper, and K.E. Muller. 1988. Applied regression analysis and other multivariable methods, 2nd ed. PWS-Kent Pub. Co., Boston, MA.

Knopf, F.L., J.A. Sedgwick, and R.W. Cannon. 1988. Guild structure of a riparian avifauna relative to seasonal cattle grazing. J. Wildl. Manage. 51: 280-290.

Krebs, C. 1989. Ecological methodology. Harper and Row, NY.

Laake, J.L., S.T. Buckland, D.R. Anderson, and K.P Burnham, 1993. DISTANCE User's Guide. Colorado Cooperative Fish & Wildl. Research Unit, Col. State Univ., Fort Collins, CO 80523.

Lancia, R.A., J.D. Nichols, and K.H. Pollock. 1996. Estimating the number of animals in wildlife populations. *In* T.A. Bookhout (ed.), Research and management techniques for wildlife and habitats, 5th ed. The Wildl. Soc., Bethesda, MD.

Larson, D.L. and C.E. Bock. 1986. Determining avian habitat preference by bird-centered vegetation sampling. *In* J. Verner, C.J. Ralph, and M.L. Morrison (eds.), Wildlife 2000: Modeling habitat relationships of terrestrial vertebrates. Univ. of Wisconsin Press, Madison, WI.

Lebreton, J.-D., K.P. Burnham, J. Clobert, and D.R. Anderson. 1992. Modeling survival and testing biological hypotheses using marked animals: a unified approach with case studies. Ecol. Monogr. 62:67-118.

Lebreton, J.-D., A.-M. Reboulet, and G. Banco. 1993. An overview of software for terrestrial vertebrate population dynamics. *In* J.-D. Lebreton, and P.M. North (eds.), Marked individuals in the study of bird populations. Birkhaeuser Verlag, Basel, Germany.

Link, W.A. and J.S. Hatfield. 1990. Power calculations and model selection for trend analysis: a comment. Ecology 71:1217-1220.

Lokemoen, J. and R. Koford. 1996. Using candlers to determine the incubation stage of passerine eggs. J. Field Ornithol. 67:660-668.

Loyn, R.H. 1986. The 20 minute search—a simple method for counting forest birds. Corella 10:58-60.

Ludwig, J.A. and J.F. Reynolds. 1988. Statistical Ecology: a primer on methods and computing. Wiley & Sons, NY.

MacArthur, R.H. 1965. Patterns of species diversity. Biol. Rev. 40:510-533.

Magurran, A.E. 1988. Ecological diversity and its measurement. Princeton Univ. Press, NJ.

Martin, T.E. 1992. Breeding productivity considerations: what are the appropriate habitat features for management? *In* J. M. Hagan and D. W. Johnston (eds.), Ecology and conservation of neotropical migrant birds. Smithson. Inst. Press, Washington, D.C.

Martin, T.E. and P. Li. 1992. Life history traits of open- vs. cavity-nesting birds. Ecology 73:579-592.

Martin, T.E. and G.R. Geupel. 1993. Nest monitoring plots: methods for locating nests and monitoring success. J. Field. Ornithol. 64:507-519.

Martin, T.E. and J.J. Roper. 1988. Nest predation and nest site selection of a western population of the Hermit Thrush. Condor 90:51-57.

Martin, T.E., J. Clobert, and D.R. Anderson. 1995. Return rates in studies of life history evolution: are biases large? J. Appl. Statistics 22:863-875.

Martin, T.E., C. Paine, C.J. Conway, W.M. Hochachka, P. Allen, and W. Jenkins. 1997. BBIRD Field Protocol. (Document available from Montana Cooperative Wildlife Research Unit, Univ. of Montana, Missoula, MT 59812; web site: http://pica.wru.umt.edu/bbird/)

Mayfield, H. 1961. Nesting success calculated from exposure. Wilson Bull. 73:255-261.

Mayfield, H. 1975. Suggestions for calculating nest success. Wilson Bull. 87:456-466.

McShea, W.J. and J.H. Rappole. 1997. Variable song rates in three species of passerines and implications for estimating bird populations. J. Field Ornithol. 68:367-375.

Neter, J., W. Wasserman and M.H. Kutner. 1990. Applied linear statistical models: regression, analysis of variance, and experimental designs, 3rd edition. Irwin, Homewood, Ill.

Noon, B.R. 1981. Techniques for sampling avian habitat. *In* D.E. Capen (ed.), The use of multivariate statistics in studies of wildlife habitat. USDA For. Serv., GTR-RM-87, Rocky Mountain Forest and Range Station, Fort Collins, CO.

Nur, N. and J. Clobert. 1988. Measuring Darwinian fitness in birds: a field guide. *In* H. Ouellet (ed.), Acta XIX Congressus Internationalis Ornithologici. Univ. of Ottawa Press, Canada.

Nur, N. and G.R. Geupel. 1993a. Validating the use of constant effort mist-netting to monitor avian populations. Unpubl. PRBO final report to U.S. Fish & Wildl. Serv. (Available from Point Reyes Bird Observatory, Stinson Beach, CA 94970).

Nur, N. and G.R. Geupel. 1993b. Evaluation of nest monitoring, mist-netting, and other methods for monitoring demographic processes in landbird populations. *In* D. M. Finch and P. W. Stangel (eds.), Status and management of neotropical migrant birds. USDA For. Serv. Publ.: GTR RM-229, Fort Collins, CO.

Nur, N., G.R. Geupel, and G. Ballard. 1994. Assessing the impact of the Cantara spill on terrestrial bird populations along the Sacramento River: Results from the 1993 field season. Unpubl. report to California Dept. of Fish and Game. (Available from Point Reyes Bird Observatory, Stinson Beach, CA 94970).

Ortega, C.P., J.C. Ortega, C.A. Rapp, S. Vorisek, S.A. Backensto, and D.W. Palmer. 1997. Effect of research activity on the success of American Robin nests. J. Wildl. Manage. 61:948-952.

Peach, W.J., S.R. Baillie, and L. Underhill. 1991. Survival of British Sedge Warblers *Acrocephalus schoenobaenus* in relation to west African rainfall. Ibis 133:300-305.

Peach, W.J. 1993. Combining mark-recapture data sets for small passerines. *In* J.-D. Lebreton and P. M. North (eds.), Marked individuals in the study of bird populations. Birkhaeuser, Basel, Germany.

Pielou, E. C. 1975. Ecological diversity. Wiley, New York.

Pollock, K.H., and W.L. Cornelius. 1988. A distribution-free nest survival model. Biometrics 44:397-404.

Pollock, K.H., J.D. Nichols, C. Brownie, and J.E. Hines. 1990. Statistical inference for capture-recapture experiments. Wildl. Monogr. 107.

Pradel, R. and J.-D. Lebreton. 1993. User's manual for program SURGE Version 4.2. CEFE/CNRS, Montpelier. (Available from J.-D. Lebreton, CEFE/CNRS, BP 5051, 34033 Montpellier Cedex, France.)

Ralph, C.J., G.R. Geupel, P. Pyle, T.E. Martin, and D.F. DeSante. 1993. Handbook of field methods for monitoring landbirds. USDA For. Serv. Publ., PSW-GTR-144, Albany, CA.

Ralph, C.J., S. Droege, and J.R. Sauer. 1995. Monitoring bird populations by point counts. USDA For. Serv. Publ., Gen. Tech. Rep. PSW-GTR-149, Albany, CA.

Ralph, C.J. and J.M. Scott. 1981. Estimating numbers of terrestrial birds. Stud. in Avian Biol., No. 6.

Ramsey, F.L. and J. M. Scott. 1981. Analysis of bird survey data using a modification of Emlen's method. *In* C. J. Ralph and J. M. Scott (eds.), Estimating numbers of terrestrial birds. Stud. in Avian Biol., No. 6.

Robinson, S.K., F.R. Thompson, T.M. Donovan, D.R. Whitehead, and J. Faaborg. 1995. Regional forest fragmentation and the nesting success of migratory birds. Science 267:1987-1990.

Sauer, J.R. 1998. Inventory methods for birds. Unpublished report to U.S. DOI National Park Serv.

Sauer, J.R. and B.K. Williams. 1989. Generalized procedures for testing hypotheses about survival or recovery rates. J. of Wildl. Manage. 53:137-142.

Skalski, J.R. and D.S. Robson. 1992. Techniques for wildlife investigations: Design and analysis of capture data. Academic Press, San Diego, CA.

Sherry, T. and R. Holmes. 1993. Are populations of neotropical migrant birds limited in summer of winter? *In* D. M. Finch and P. W. Stangel (eds.), Status and management of neotropical migrant birds. USDA For. Serv. Publ.: GTR RM-229, Fort Collins, CO.

Silkey, M., N. Nur and G.R. Geupel. 1999. Can mist nets track annual variation in abundance? A validation study. Condor.

Slater, P.J. 1994. Factors affecting the efficiency of the area search method of censusing birds in open forests and woodlands. Emu 94:9-16.

Snedecor, G.W. and W.G. Cochran. 1989. Statistical methods, 8th edition. Iowa State Univ. Press, Ames.

Spear, L. and N. Nur. 1994. Brood size, hatching order and hatching date: effects on four life-history stages from hatching to recruitment in western gulls. J. of Animal Ecol. 63:283-298.

Sokal, R.R. and F.J. Rohlf. 1995. Biometry: the principles and practice of statistics in biological research, 3rd ed. W. H. Freeman, San Francisco, CA

StataCorp. 1999. Stata Statistical Software, Release 6.0. Stata Corporation, College Station, TX.

Sydeman, W.J., H.R. Huber, S.D. Emslie, C.A. Ribic, and N. Nur. 1991. Age-specific weaning success of Northern elephant seals in relation to previous breeding experience. Ecology 72:2204-2217.

Thomas, L. and C.J. Krebs. 1997. A review of statistical power analysis software. Bull. Ecol. Soc. of Am. 78:126-138.

Thomas, L. 1996. Monitoring long-term population change: why are there so many analysis methods? Ecology 71:49-58.

Trexler, J.C. and J. Travis. 1993. Nontraditional regression analyses. Ecology 74:1629-1637.

Verner, J. 1985. Assessment of counting techniques. Current Ornithol. 2:247-301.

Verner, J. and T. A. Larson. 1989. Richness of breeding bird species in mixed-conifer forest of the Sierra Nevada, CA. Auk 106:447-461.

White, G.C. 1986. Program SURVIV user's manual, version 1.2. Dept. of Fishery and Wild. Biol., Colorado State Univ., Fort Collins.

White, G.C., D.R. Anderson, K.P. Burnham, and D.L. Otis. 1982. Capture-recapture and removal method for sampling closed population. Los Alamos National Laboratory, LA-8787-NERP.

Zar, J.H. 1996. Biostatistical analysis, 3rd ed. Prentice-Hall, Inc., Englewood Cliffs, NJ

Notes and Calculations

U.S. Department of the Interior
U.S. Fish & Wildlife Service

http://www.fws.gov